DRESSED BY THE BEST

WEARABLE ART PROJECTS
BY 10 WELL-KNOWN DESIGNERS

That Patchwork Place®

Credits

Editor-in-Chief	Kerry I. Smith
Technical Editor	Barbara Weiland
Managing Editor	Judy Petry
Design Director	Cheryl Stevenson
Cover Designer	Magrit Baurecht
Text Designer	Amy Shayne
Production Assistant	Marijane E. Figg
Copy Editor	Liz McGehee
Proofreader	Tina Cook
Illustrator	Robin Strobel
Photographer	Brent Kane

Dressed by the Best: Wearable Art Projects by 10 Well-Known Designers
© 1997 by That Patchwork Place, Inc.
PO Box 118, Bothell, WA 98041-0118 USA

Printed in Hong Kong
02 01 00 99 98 97   6 5 4 3 2 1

Library of Congress Cataloging-in-Publication Data

Dressed by the best: wearable art projects by 10 well-known designers.
  p. cm.
  ISBN 1-56477-196-2
  1. Patchwork—Patterns. 2. Appliqué. 3 Wearable art. I. That Patchwork Place, Inc.
TT835.D73 1997
746.46'0432—dc21   97-25263
                                                    CIP

Table of Contents

Introduction

If you love to wear your fiber art on your back, you may have difficulty choosing which of these ten terrific wearable art projects to make first. Each project was hand picked by the acquisitions editors at That Patchwork Place from a variety of intriguing garments and accessories submitted for review. Each one is appropriate for many body types and sizes, and the techniques represented are easily adapted to other garment types and styles. With a shopping list and complete step-by-step directions for each project, you'll be able to sew your way to a beautiful piece of wearable art—even if you've never attempted such a project before.

If you've always wanted to know how a designer approaches the design process to create an interesting garment, turn to "Check it Out" on page 84. Designer Lorraine Torrence shares her process, using her colorful ensemble as an example only. Once you've read through her guidelines, you will have enough know-how to create your own one-of-a-kind garment.

In a similar vein, Mary Mashuta shares general directions for creating pieced fabric you can use to cut and assemble an allover pieced jacket or vest. "Irma's Stripes" on page 46 features an intriguing Origami Triangle block, but you can interchange other geometric blocks, following Mary's planning and piecing advice.

If you're not quite ready to design your own project, you'll find all the information you need for making your version of the remaining seven garments—and one colorful coin purse, which Janet Carija Brandt does in wool-on-wool appliqué on page 54.

Since vests and tunics are easy to sew and fun to wear, you'll find several included in this book. If you love the look of sashiko, the traditional hand quilting of Japan, you'll enjoy imitating it by machine on the simple garment on page 30, "Sashiko Bolero," designed by Shirley Miller Holmes. It's much faster when stitched in this manner, and you can even incorporate some of the built-in decorative stitches on your machine.

Judy Bishop's "Fiesta Vest" on page 6 features eyelash appliqué—an interesting, easy-to-do technique that adds textural interest to simple shapes. The resulting work looks like complex tile work, belying the simplicity of the method.

Lois Ericson's "Woven Puzzle Vest" on page 38 is a puzzle of woven fabric strips shrouded in a sheer fabric for an unusual, elegant treatment. You'll love trying Lois's unique front closure too.

If appliqué is your thing, check out the "Elegant Tunic" on page 60 by Maggie Walker. The reversible, long vest features her unique method of combining floral appliqué collage with thread painting. Virginia Avery's colorful "Red Alert" on page 14 presents a similar method for making a great-looking, easy-to-sew reversible jacket.

For a simple, yet elegant wearable project, use two hand-dyed silk scarves to make Betty Kershner's "Scarf Kimono" on page 24. It's an easy project with great panache to wear over a plain silk dress or top and pants.

Weave it, trim it, scrunch it, pleat it. If you love embellishment and unique textures, you'll love Grace France's unique vest jacket, "Love of Life, Love of Color," on page 72. Colorful pin-woven sleeves, created with textured-fabric techniques, attach to a simple vest shape of your choosing. Grace also includes some great ideas for the usual and not-so-usual embellishments to inspire you to use those pretty treasures you've been collecting.

So, take a few minutes to look through the projects in this book, then choose your favorite garment or technique and try your hand at creating your own unique garment. You'll make a statement when you wear it, and the compliments will surely send you back to your machine to make another one of these wonderful projects.

Happy sewing!

Barbara Weiland

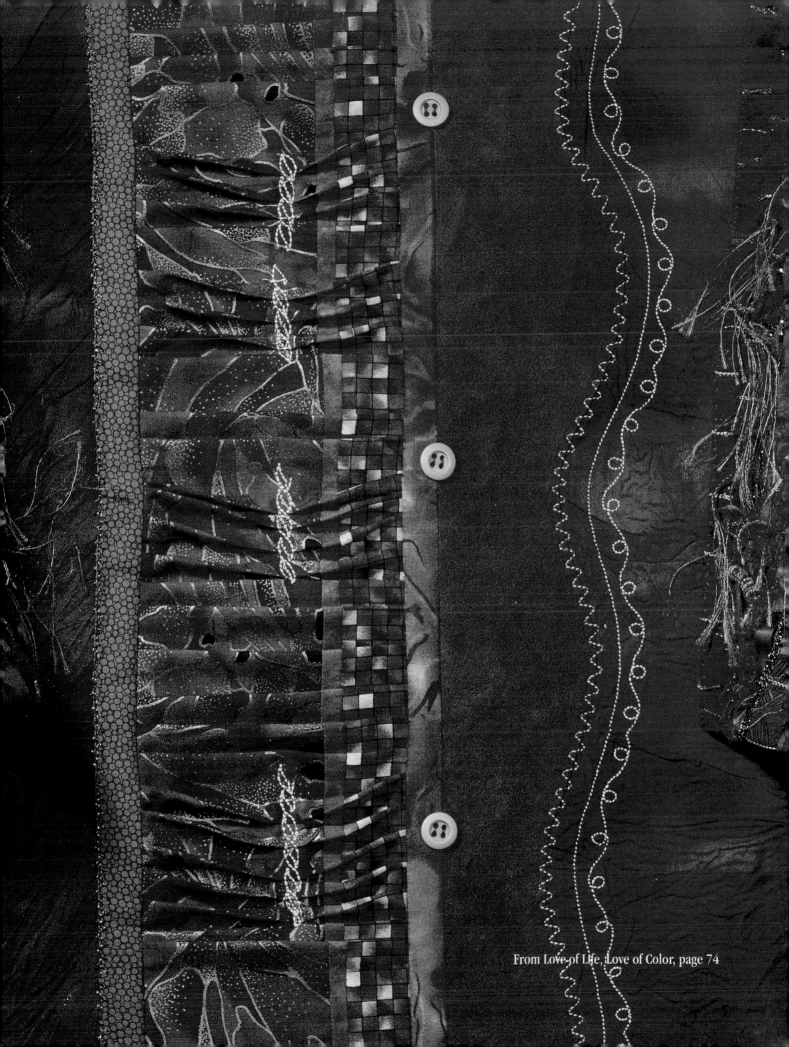

From Love of Life, Love of Color, page 74

Fiesta Vest

BY JUDY BISHOP

Embellished with colorful fringed shapes and multicolor piping, this simple vest offers a place to experiment with color and design while creating a fun garment to wear. The possibilities are endless; once you know how to make and apply the eyelash appliqué, you'll find it easy to use this technique on other garments of your own design.

Meet Judy Bishop

Judy Bishop's interest in clothing design began as a child when she used strips of fabric to create things for her clothespin dolls to wear. Her passion for fabric led to bachelor's and master's degrees in home economics with an emphasis in textiles and clothing. After thirteen years as a college instructor, she "retired" to pursue her dream of publishing and marketing patterns for her unique garment designs, which beautifully combine her love for textiles and her knowledge of needle-art techniques. She specially designs the garment shapes to include areas for embellishment. Judy has continued her teaching as a freelance instructor for more than ten years.

Judy's artistic garments have received many awards and have been juried into exhibitions throughout the United States and internationally. In 1992, Judy was a featured designer in "Designers Across America," published in *NeedleArts* magazine. She launched her pattern line, "from the Judy Bishop Collection" in 1994, and in 1995 her teaching project, "The Victorian Patchwork Vest," appeared as a segment on the cable TV program *The Embroidery Studio*. Several of her garments have appeared in magazines, including *Sew News*, *McCall's Quilting*, and *American Quilter*.

The eyelash technique featured in this project was the result of Judy's experimentation with hand-loomed Guatemalan cottons, which are easy to unravel. Working with the intriguing self-fringed shapes led her to try the more readily available Kona Cotton solids. Beautiful, thick "eyelashes" form when the Kona Cottons are unraveled, due to their heavy yarns and even weave. The fringed appliquéd shapes on a darker base fabric resemble the look of mosaic tile work, with the garment fabric providing the "grout" between shapes.

Judy lives in Carson, California, with her husband, Ron. She continues to give lectures and presentations on her favorite subject—making wearable art—and is enjoying her new role as grandmother.

Fiesta Vest
by Judy Bishop, Carson, California, 1996.

Fiesta Vest
(back view)

Eyelash detail

Shopping List

Note: Yardage in parentheses is for XL and XXL sizes.

Panel Vest, View B, by Judy Bishop Designs*

1 yd. (1¼ yds.) black cotton for vest base fabric

¾ yd. (1 yd.) fine-quality muslin for underlining

⅛ yd. each of 8 different colors of Kona Cotton solids** for eyelash appliqués

¾ yd. (1 yd.) black lining fabric

¾ yd. (1 yd.) medium-weight fusible interfacing

4 yds. cotton cording for piping

Thread to match base fabric

Open-toe appliqué or embroidery presser foot

Piping foot, beading foot, or zipper foot

Size 70 sewing-machine needle

Chalk pencil

Optional: Piping or beading foot

* *Look for this pattern at your local fabric/quilt shop or see page 95 for ordering information. You can use a similarly styled commercial vest pattern; however, you may need to adapt the pattern and adjust yardages.*

** *Kona Cotton solids are recommended because the heavier yarns in this fabric make wonderful fringed edges on the appliqués. Substitute a similar cotton if necessary; hand-woven fabrics, such as Guatemalan cottons, are also appropriate for the appliqués.*

Preparation and Cutting

1. Wash the muslin to preshrink. Press to remove wrinkles. *Do not wash the eyelash fabrics.*

2. Using the vest pattern pieces for your size, cut 2 front panels, 1 back panel, and 2 side front panels from the vest base fabric, underlining fabric, and lining fabric. Cut the front bands and corresponding interfacing, following the pattern directions.

3. Remove the pattern pieces and place each piece of underlining on the wrong side of a corresponding piece of base fabric. Smooth in place, making sure all raw edges are even. It may be necessary to trim the underlining to match the base fabric layer. Treat the two layers as one, using only a few pins to hold them together for the next steps.

4. Cut a 22"-long piece from each of the 8 appliqué fabrics and set aside for the multicolor piping. You may layer as many as 4 of these fabrics together to make the cuts. From each remaining appliqué fabric, cut 1 square, 2½" x 2½", for the large eyelash triangles. Refer to the cutting diagrams on the facing page.

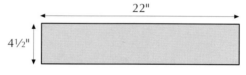

22"

4½"

Reserve for multicolor piping.

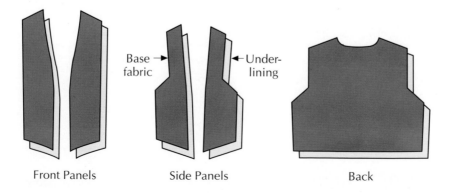

Front Panels   Base fabric →   ← Under-lining   Side Panels   Back

5. From the remaining appliqué fabrics, cut a variety of rectangles and squares, varying them from ½" to 1¼" wide. It is best to first cut a strip of the desired width, and then cut the strip into squares and rectangles as shown in the bottom two diagrams. Cut shapes from each color as you need them. The number of shapes you cut is dictated by your final arrangement of shapes and the vest size you are making.

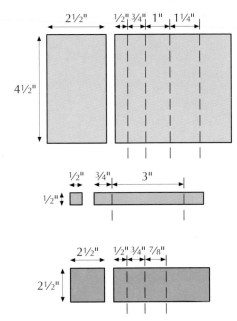

Assembling the Vest

1. With the base fabric facing up, use a chalk pencil to mark ½"-wide seam allowances on the vest front pieces. The vest fronts should be lying side by side during the design process.

2. Place 3 of the 2½" squares on-point along the outside edges of 1 front panel. Place 4 squares on the other front panel.

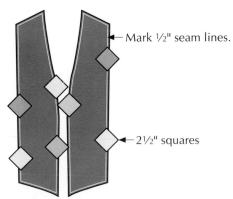

— Mark ½" seam lines.

— 2½" squares

3. Arrange the appliqué shapes as desired on 1 vest front, leaving approximately ¼" of space between the individual units and placing the straight edges at a 45° angle to the front edge. Use the edges of the on-point squares as a guide. Repeat on the other vest front. (*You will fringe the pieces after finalizing the appliqué arrangement.*) Examine the arrangement for color balance, spacing between shapes, and color repeats that are too close together. Adjust the shapes and the design as necessary.

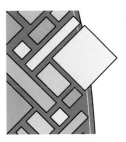

4. To fringe each appliqué, remove 6 to 8 threads from each edge so the resulting fringe is ⅛" wide all around. As you complete the fringing on a unit, reposition it on the vest front and use a straight pin to secure it.

5. Adjust the sewing machine for a short, narrow zigzag stitch (stitch length: 1mm; stitch width: 1.5mm). Attach an open-toe appliqué or embroidery foot. Thread the machine with thread to match the vest fabric.

6. Stitch each appliqué in place, beginning at one end of the vest piece and working to the other. Remove pins as you finish each appliqué. You may need to reposition some pins during stitching. To stitch the appliqués in place, dial down to an almost 0 stitch length and take 3 or 4 tiny stitches; then readjust to a stitch length of 1mm and zigzag each shape in place, making sure the needle enters the base fabric just beyond the last woven thread in the appliqué on the right-hand swing of the needle to prevent any further raveling. The needle must also enter the base fabric at each corner so you can pivot and continue stitching. To end the stitching on each shape, dial down to an almost 0 stitch length and take a few stitches. Clip all threads close to the surface of the work. Trim the large squares even with the vest front cut edges.

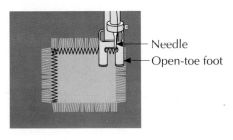

— Needle
— Open-toe foot

7. On the vest back, position one square on the upper left armhole and the other one on the bottom right edge as shown. Use appliqué shapes to create an upper (yoke) and lower design area, referring to the diagram for placement ideas. Fringe and stitch the shapes in place as directed for the vest fronts.

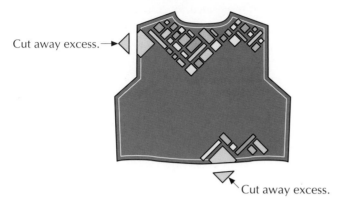

8. Press each completed vest piece.
9. Trim ½" from each long edge of each neckband interfacing piece. Apply interfacing to the wrong side of the neckbands. With right sides together, stitch the center back seam ½" from the raw edges. Press the seam open.

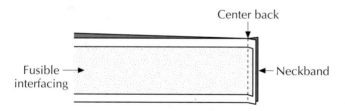

10. Make multicolor piping, following the directions in the sidebar on page 13.

11. Pin the piping to the right side of one long edge of the neckband. Machine baste in place with raw edges even, using a piping or beading foot. (If you do not have a piping or beading foot, use a zipper foot with a contrasting-color thread in the bobbin and baste in place.) Pin and machine baste piping to the long straight edge of each side front panel in the same manner.

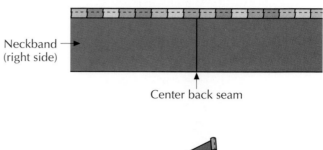

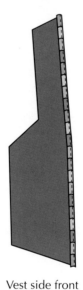

Vest side front

12. Complete the vest, following the pattern directions. When stitching the side front panels and the front band to the vest front, use the piping or beading foot. (If using a zipper foot instead, stitch from the side with contrasting basting, stitching just inside the basting.)

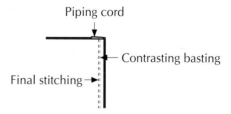

Multicolor Piping

1. For the XS and S vest sizes, cut 1 strip, 1½" wide, from each of the reserved 22"-long strips of appliqué fabrics and sew the strips together, using ¼"-wide seams and *alternating the sewing direction to prevent the resulting panel from bowing. Press all seams open.* For all other sizes, cut 2 strips from each fabric and make 2 pieced panels.

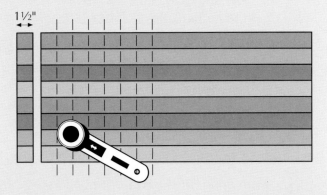

2. Cut 1½"-wide strips from the pieced panel(s). Sew the strips together to make one continuous strip the length of the neckband. Sew the remaining strips together to make 2 strips, each long enough for a side front vest panel.

3. Wrap each pieced strip around the cording, right side out, and machine baste, using the piping, beading, or zipper foot to stitch close to the cording. When using a piping or beading foot, adjust the needle position 2 positions to the right. For the final garment construction step, move the needle 1 position to the right of center so the first stitching will not show.

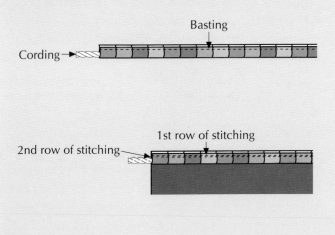

Red Alert

BY VIRGINIA AVERY

This eye-catching little jacket with turn-back lapels and cuffs captures Virginia Avery's sense of whimsy and her talent for combining color and fabric in imaginative ways. The simply styled fire-engine-red jacket reverses to a dynamic black print. Appliqués, "sandwich stitching," and graphic black-and-white binding make this an appealing project, which is deceivingly simple to make—completely by machine. It's the perfect first wearables project for the beginner. A pattern is provided on the pullout page for the add-on lapels if you cannot find a similarly styled commercial pattern.

Virginia considers red her personal neutral—a basic necessity in her wardrobe. She also believes that a jacket is the primary clothing item for personal expression in any woman's wardrobe.

Meet Virginia Avery

Virginia Avery is a well-known figure in quilt and wearable-art circles. A dynamic sense of design and the uncanny ability to turn something simple into something smashing characterizes her work. A pioneer in the quilt world with more than twenty-five years of work to her credit, Virginia is a sought-after teacher. Her lecture circuit has spanned many continents, and she is known for sharing her enthusiasm and her knowledge without reserve.

Besides making quilts and wearables and teaching classes about them, Virginia judges, lectures, and writes. She is known as the quilt world's strongest advocate for wearable art, and she is the author of several books. In addition, her writing and work have appeared in numerous magazine articles.

Warmth and wit characterize everything Virginia does, and her fiber art is represented in many private and public collections. Most recently, her work was included in Nihon Vogue's exquisite book, *88 Leaders in the Quilt World*. She has numerous one-woman shows to her credit and recently completed her fourteenth garment for the famous Fairfield Fashion Show.

In her spare time, Virginia plays piano (without printed music!) for an eight-member Dixieland jazz band. She firmly believes that contemporary quilting and jazz are sisters under the skin because they both require improvising on a theme. Virginia's love for jazz shows in her work, and she sometimes names her garments for favorite jazz tunes.

In 1996, Virginia was the recipient of the coveted Silver Star Award at the International Quilt Festival in Houston for her extraordinary contributions to quilting. It's a most fitting tribute to add to her list of accomplishments, which include the Distinguished Alumnus Award from her alma mater, DePauw University, and being named as one of the 1000 most influential women of the '90s by *Mirabella* magazine.

Red Alert
by Virginia Avery, Port Chester, New York, 1996.

Lapel detail

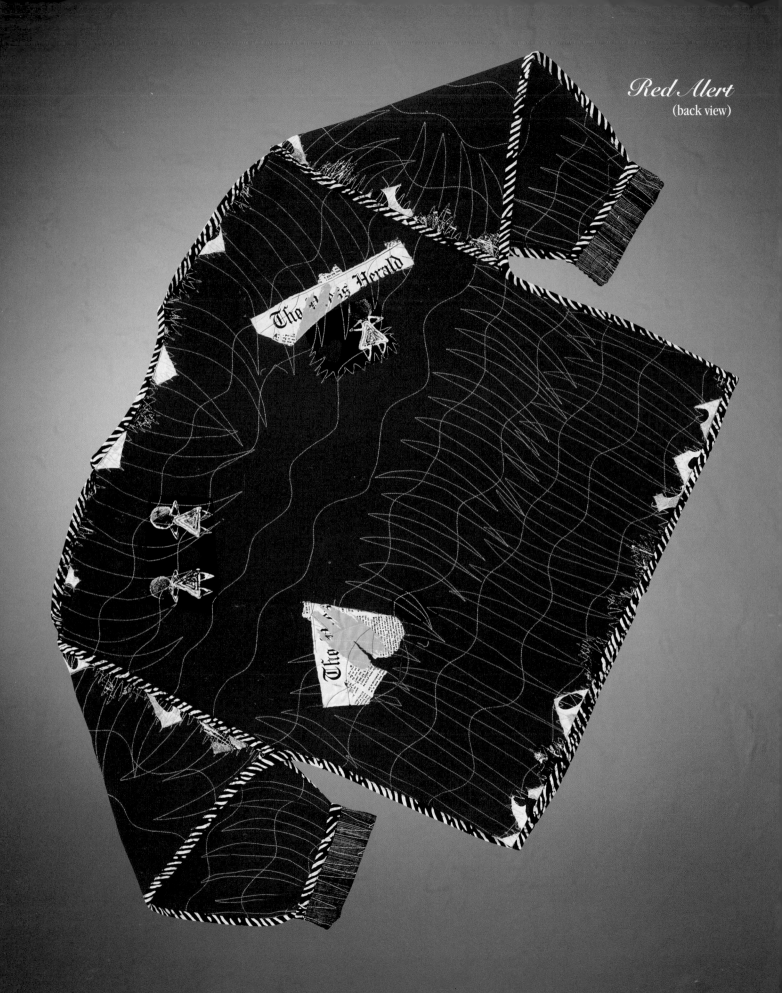

Red Alert
Reversed (front view)

Lapel detail

Shopping List

Note: *Plus sizes may require additional yardage.*

Simple jacket pattern with dropped armhole sleeves and no darts*
Fabric of your choice for outer shell**
Contrasting, coordinating fabric for reverse side of jacket**
Muslin or cotton flannel for foundation**
Scraps of unusual, eye-catching fabrics for appliqués and half-square triangles
¾ yd. black-and-white fabric for Hong Kong binding and slot pockets
Metallic, rayon, and regular sewing threads
Optional: Pattern tracing cloth or tracing paper

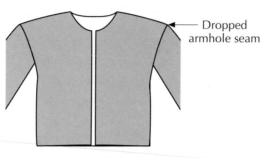

Dropped armhole seam

Straight front

* *If you cannot find a similar pattern with lapels like the one shown, look for a jacket pattern with a straight front-button closure you can adapt, following the directions and diagrams in "Preparation and Cutting." The diagram above shows the general shaping to look for when selecting a pattern. A dropped shoulder requiring a flat sleeve cap is essential. The sleeve should have a shape similar to the one in the illustration at the top of page 20.*

** *Refer to yardage chart on pattern envelope.*

Preparation and Cutting

Note: *The lapel pattern is on the pullout page.*

1. To add lapels to your jacket pattern, trace the lapel pattern onto pattern tracing cloth or tracing paper. If necessary, adjust the length of the lapel to fit your pattern by taking a tuck in it or slashing and spreading it, then reshaping as necessary. Lap the straight edge over the pattern *at the front seam line*. If your jacket has a front-button closure, turn the front edge (the overlap portion) under along the center front line, then butt the lapel pattern up to it. Draw in a smooth transition from the neckline curve to the lapel as needed.

Triangles indicate suggested placement for triangle appliqués.

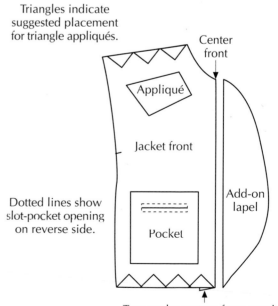

Center front

Appliqué

Jacket front

Dotted lines show slot-pocket opening on reverse side.

Pocket

Add-on lapel

Turn under pattern front overlap before adding lapel.

2. For the patch pocket, draw a pattern piece 8½" x 9".

3. For the two-piece sleeve, draw a straight line, parallel to the grain line, from the shoulder dot to the bottom edge. Cut the sleeve into two pieces along the line. Trace each sleeve half onto pattern tracing cloth or tracing paper and add ½"-wide seam allowances to each cut edge. Be sure to label each piece accurately, remembering that the back armhole has 2 notches, the front only 1.

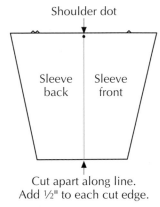

Shoulder dot

Sleeve back | Sleeve front

Cut apart along line.
Add ½" to each cut edge.

4. Use the jacket back pattern piece and the new pattern pieces for the jacket front and the front and back sleeves to cut the required pieces from all 3 fabrics: the outer layer, the muslin or flannel foundation, and the inner layer. Remove the pattern pieces and make a fabric sandwich for each jacket piece, placing the foundation layer between the fashion fabrics. Pin the layers together for the following construction method.

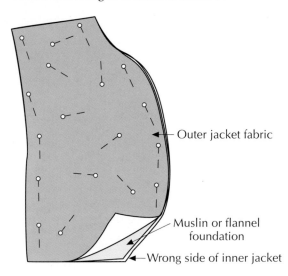

Outer jacket fabric

Muslin or flannel foundation

Wrong side of inner jacket

Constructing the Jacket

Note: *Treat all three layers of the fabric sandwich as one during jacket construction.*

1. Referring to the "Red Alert" jacket photos for inspiration, cut several appliqué shapes of the desired size for the outer jacket. It is not necessary to add a turn-under allowance because the edges are left raw. Heavy stitching over the appliqués to secure them and to quilt the sandwich layers together will keep the appliqués from raveling. Position the appliqués on the jacket fronts and back as desired and pin in place.

2. Cut 2" squares from a variety of fabrics. Cut each square in half diagonally for half-square triangles. Position them along the front and back shoulder-seam edges, the upper edge of each sleeve piece, and the bottom edge of the jacket fronts and back. Refer to the jacket photos. Pin in place. Position as desired on each patch pocket. They do not have to match.

Patch pocket

3. Thread the machine with the desired thread(s). Stitch each jacket section heavily, referring to the diagrams for stitch-pattern possibilities and to the jacket photo for stitch placement. Stitch the patch pockets in the same manner.

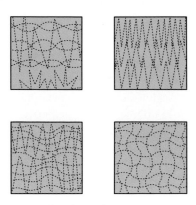

Sandwich stitching patterns

4. With raw edges even and the reverse sides of the fabric sandwich together, pin each front sleeve to a back sleeve. Cut a 1¾"-wide bias strip from the binding fabric, and pin in place on top, right sides together. Stitch ½" from the raw edges. Trim the seam to ⅜", *making sure it is an even width along the entire length of the seam.*

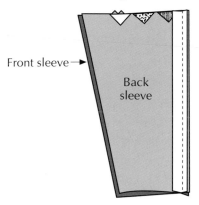

Front sleeve →

Back sleeve

Stitch ½" from raw edges;
trim to ⅜".

5. Press the bias strip toward the trimmed seam allowance, then wrap it to the underside of the seam and pin in place. Stitch in-the-ditch of the previous seam to secure the underside of the bias, then trim the excess close to the stitching. Since the strip is cut on the bias, it won't ravel.

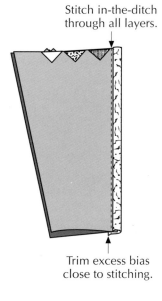

Stitch in-the-ditch
through all layers.

Trim excess bias
close to stitching.

6. With wrong sides together, stitch the jacket shoulder seams with a 1¾"-wide bias strip cut from the binding fabric. Stitch and finish as directed for the sleeve seam.

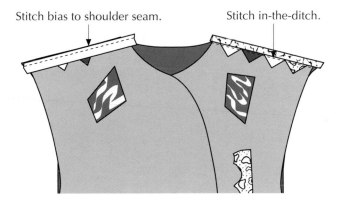

Stitch bias to shoulder seam.

Stitch in-the-ditch.

Designer Tip

If you don't like the raw edge of the binding:

1. Cut 3"-wide true-bias strips for the binding. Join short strips to make one strip long enough for the total amount of binding required.
2. Fold the binding strip in half lengthwise, wrong sides together, and press lightly.
3. Pin the binding to the garment with raw edges aligned and stitch ½" from the raw edges. Trim the seam to an even ⅜". Turn the bias strip over the raw edge and hand stitch in place.

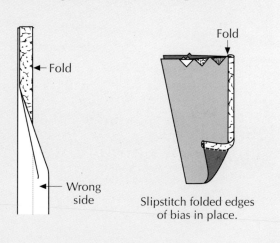

Fold

Fold

← Fold

Wrong
side

Slipstitch folded edges
of bias in place.

7. Pin a sleeve to each armhole with the reverse side of the fabric sandwich right sides together, the shoulder dot at the shoulder seam, and the front and back armhole notches matching. Turn the bound sleeve seam toward the jacket back, and the bound shoulder seam toward the jacket front to avoid a lump where they meet. Pin a binding strip in place as you did for the previous seams. Stitch and finish as directed for the sleeve seam.

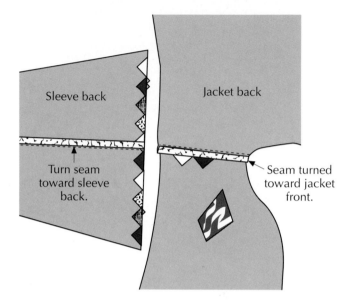

8. To finish the edges of the patch pocket, apply a bias strip of binding to the right side of the pocket on all 4 edges, mitering the corners as shown. Stitch ⅜" from the raw edges.

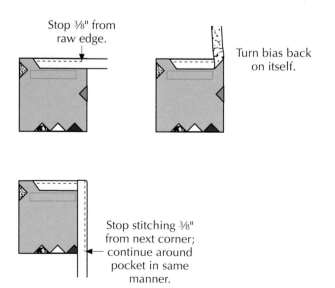

Stop ⅜" from raw edge.

Turn bias back on itself.

Stop stitching ⅜" from next corner; continue around pocket in same manner.

Turn the binding to the underside of the pocket and stitch in-the-ditch along the top edge only of each pocket. Pin the binding in place around the remaining 3 edges on each pocket. You will complete the binding later.

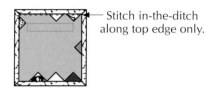

Stitch in-the-ditch along top edge only.

9. Position but do not pin the patch pockets on the right side of the jacket. Use straight pins to outline their location on each front. Remove the pockets.

On the inside of the jacket, mark the slot-pocket openings, being sure to position them at least 1½" below the marking for the top edge of the patch pockets. The pocket openings should be 5¾" long, centered within the pocket area.

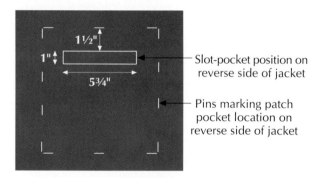

1½"

1"

5¾"

Slot-pocket position on reverse side of jacket

Pins marking patch pocket location on reverse side of jacket

10. To make the slot pocket, cut a 4" x 8" straight-grain rectangle from the binding fabric. Draw a 1" x 5¾" rectangle on the wrong side, centering it in the fabric rectangle. Place the rectangle in position, face down on the reverse side of the jacket, and pin in place. Using 18 to 20 stitches per inch, stitch on the marked lines. Slash through the center and out to the corners, being careful not to clip the stitches at the corners.

Start stitching on one long edge, not at a corner.

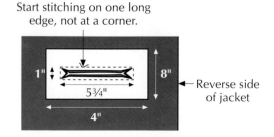

1"

5¾"

8"

4"

Reverse side of jacket

11. Pull the fabric rectangle through the opening and create 2 pocket welts by making ½"-wide folds in the rectangle under the opening. Pin. Turn the garment away from the welts and stitch across the triangle at each end to secure them.

Fold in two ½"-wide welts in the pocket opening.

Stitch across triangle to secure pocket welts.

12. Stitch in-the-ditch around the welts on the right side of the pocket opening.

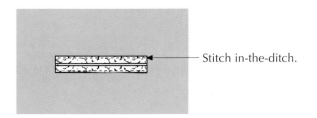

Stitch in-the-ditch.

13. Position the patch pockets on the right side of the jacket fronts and pin in place, being careful to place the already bound and stitched edge at the top. Stitch in-the-ditch on the remaining 3 edges of each pocket to secure. Backstitch at the beginning and end of the stitching.

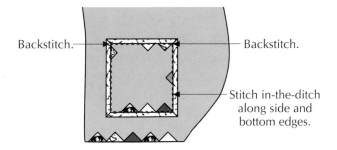

Backstitch.

Backstitch.

Stitch in-the-ditch along side and bottom edges.

14. Stitch and bind the side and sleeve underarm seam as you did the previous seams.

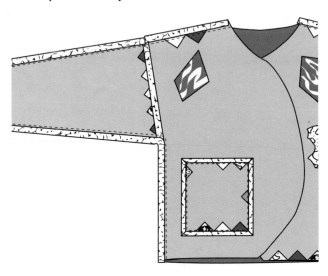

15. Cut two 1¾"-wide bias strips, each 1" or 2" longer than the circumference of the lower edge of the sleeve. Turn under and press ¼" on each strip as shown. Pin and stitch a bias strip to the right side of each sleeve, using a ⅜"-wide seam allowance. Trim away the excess. Turn the binding toward the seam and then over the seam edge to the inside. Stitch in-the-ditch from the right side and trim the excess close to the stitching line on the inside. Bind the bottom and the front and back neckline edges in the same manner, beginning and ending the bias on the bottom edge at a side seam.

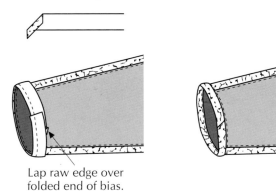

Lap raw edge over folded end of bias.

16. Turn up the sleeves to create a cuff of the desired width.

Scarf *Kimono*

BY BETTY KERSHNER

Nothing could be simpler to sew or easier to wear than this elegant kimono made from two large, hand-painted silk chiffon scarves. A solid-colored silk neckband and back panel add contrast and design interest to the simple shape. Using already hemmed silk scarves means you need to make only one short hem, sew two side seams, and attach the neckband—the perfect make-it-today, wear-it-tonight project. If you don't want to use scarves, directions are included for making the kimono from a soft, drapable fabric. If you wish, make a matching soft belt tie to cinch it in at the waist as shown in the front view photo.

Meet Betty Kershner

Betty Kershner had already tried her hand at almost every craft before she discovered fabric dyeing in 1973. Finding this process immensely satisfying, she has been painting fabrics and sewing them ever since. A member of the Southern Highland Crafts Guild based in Asheville, North Carolina, Betty conducts occasional workshops on fabric painting.

The "Scarf Kimono" is one of several one-size-fits-almost-all patterns Betty has developed to showcase her beautiful hand-painted fabrics. It is simply elegant in painted silk, but works equally well in soft, drapable fabrics, such as rayon challis.

Betty lives on a mountain plateau in Tennessee with her husband, Bill. From her second-story studio, she can see thirty miles down a cove (southern for "valley") into Alabama. She enjoys the view of sun, shadow, and mist—a theme apparent in her artistic combinations of paint colors on silk.

Betty does custom orders, particularly for weddings and reunions. Besides hangings, pieced pillows, and table runners, she also makes liturgical stoles and banners. She is the mother of two and a proud new grandmother.

Scarf Kimono
by Betty Kershner, Sewanee, Tennessee, 1996.

Shopping List

2 hand-painted silk chiffon scarves, each 22" x 72"*

OR

2 yds. of 45"-wide soft, drapable fabric

⅔ yd. of 45"-wide soft, drapable fabric in a contrasting solid color for back panel and neckband**

Note: *For information on hand painting silk, refer to one of the following books— my favorite references:*

Kennedy, Jill, and Jane Varrall, *Silk Painting: Ideas and Textures.* Radnor, Pa.: Chilton Book Co., 1992.

Kennedy, Jill, and Jane Varrall, *Silk Painting: New Ideas and Textures.* London: B. T. Batsford Ltd., 1993.

* *If this size is unavailable, make your own scarves from hand-painted or printed yardage and finish one long edge and both short ends of each piece by hand or machine, or serge a narrow, rolled hem.*

** *⅔ yd. is enough if you can cut the pieces from the fabric width; if you must cut from the fabric length, you will need 1 ¼ yds.*

Cutting and Assembling the Kimono

Note: *This kimono is generously sized—not a problem for most figure types. However, if you are petite, you may wish to scale it down a bit as indicated in parentheses in the cutting directions.*

1. Press the silk scarves to remove wrinkles. If you wish to substitute fabric yardage for the scarves, cut 2 lengths, each 22" x 72" (or 20" x 64" for petites), from the desired fabric and make a narrow rolled hem along the center 18" on one long edge of each piece.

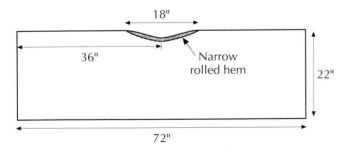

2. From the contrasting fabric, cut 2 pieces, each 6" x 45" (or 6" x 41" for petites), for the neckband, and 1 piece, 9" x 36", for the back panel.

3. Turn under and press ¼" at one short end of the back panel. Turn under again and machine stitch close to the inner fold, or hand stitch a narrow hem if you prefer.

4. At the other short end of the back panel, shape the neckline by cutting as shown. Make a ⅛"-long snip at the center of the panel neckline.

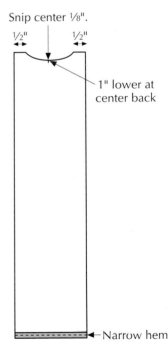

Cut 1 of contrasting fabric.

Narrow French Seam

1. Place the pieces *wrong sides together* and stitch ¼" from the raw edges. Press the seam open to set the stitches, then press the raw edges together again.
2. Trim the seam allowance to ⅛".
3. With right sides together, stitch ¼" from the first stitching line. Press the seam to one side.

Place fabric pieces wrong sides together.

Right side

Stitch ¼" from raw edges.

Press seam open.

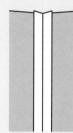

Trim to ⅛".

Wrong side

Stitch ¼" from seamed edge.

5. With right sides together, serge the back panel to one long edge of each scarf, or use a French seam (see the sidebar). Press the seams toward the scarf panels.

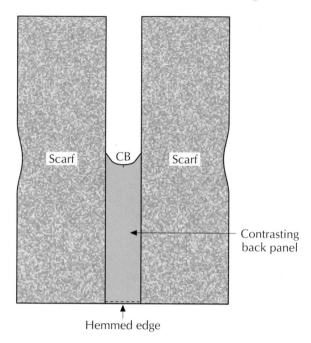

Scarf   CB   Scarf

Contrasting back panel

Hemmed edge

6. With right sides together, stitch the neckbands together at the center back, using a ¼"-wide seam allowance. Press the seam open.

Sew ¼" from center back edge of neckbands.

7. Measure from the center back snip mark to the front bottom edge of one scarf. Cut each half of the neckband to match this measurement plus ¼". Fold the band in half lengthwise with right sides together and stitch ¼" from the raw edges at each short end of the band. Turn right side out and press.

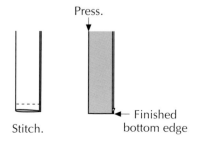

Press.

Stitch.

Finished bottom edge

8. *For a serged seam,* pin the neckband to the kimono neckline with right sides together and the center back seam at the center back snip mark. Serge and press the seam toward the kimono. *For a French seam,* pin the band to the *wrong* side of the kimono and follow the directions in the sidebar on page 28. Press the finished seam toward the kimono.

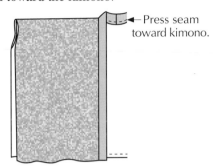

Press seam toward kimono.

9. *If you are using scarves,* fold them in half crosswise with right sides together. Stitch just inside the hemmed rolled edge, leaving a 9" opening for the armhole on each side. Use a zipper foot or piping foot to stitch just to the left of the scarf hems. *If you are using yardage* instead of scarves, serge or machine stitch a narrow side seam.

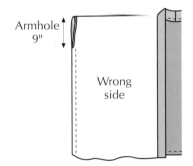

Armhole 9"

Wrong side

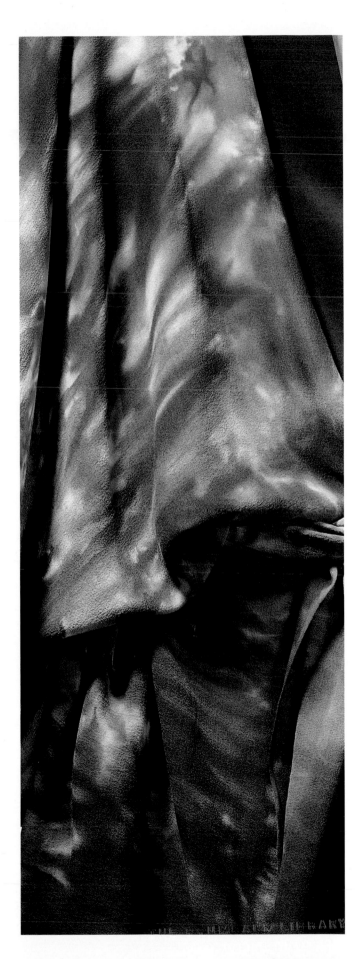

Sashiko Bolero

BY SHIRLEY MILLER HOLMES

This waist-length green denim bolero opens at the sides for easy on-and-off dressing. Embroidered with three traditional sashiko patterns sewn by machine, it requires only a long straight stitch adjusted to imitate hand stitching. The stylized landscape design was inspired by a kimono. An enamel pin on the right front shoulder sets the tone for Shirley's bolero, but the bird, fan, hearts, circle, and fish designs pictured on the pullout page are typical folk-art alternatives for this location. They can be enhanced with French knots, beads, buttons, or bows.

Meet Shirley Miller Holmes

Shirley Holmes fell in love with sashiko several years ago when she saw a dark blue denim suit embellished with a variety of geometric patterns. The patterns were stitched with heavy white thread in a long, straight machine stitch. She just had to try it. Her very first garment won Second-in-Show and a top-of-the-line serger in a 1993 national contest! Since then, she has earned further recognition teaching and creating exciting sashiko outfits and accessories. She has also developed new ways to draw traditional patterns with her specially designed templates.

Shirley likes to sew quilts and clothes that are elegant in their simplicity—projects that are quick, easy, and fun to make. The structured geometrics of sashiko are clean and simple, yet they leave lots of room for creativity: you must still choose the patterns and arrange them on a project; select threads, fabrics, beads, and trim; and find the built-in machine stitches that enhance the designs, yet remain in keeping with sashiko tradition and the aesthetics of Japanese textile art.

While raising five children, living and traveling overseas with her husband, and teaching college English, Shirley found time to use her college major in clothing and textiles to teach adult-education and children's sewing classes. She earned a master's degree after the birth of her fourth child.

Shirley lives in Sewanee, Tennessee, where she studies Japanese textile art, creates new sashiko projects, makes doll clothes, quilts, teaches, and takes all the sewing lessons she can "to make my computerized sewing machines talk to me and give added dimension to my sashiko."

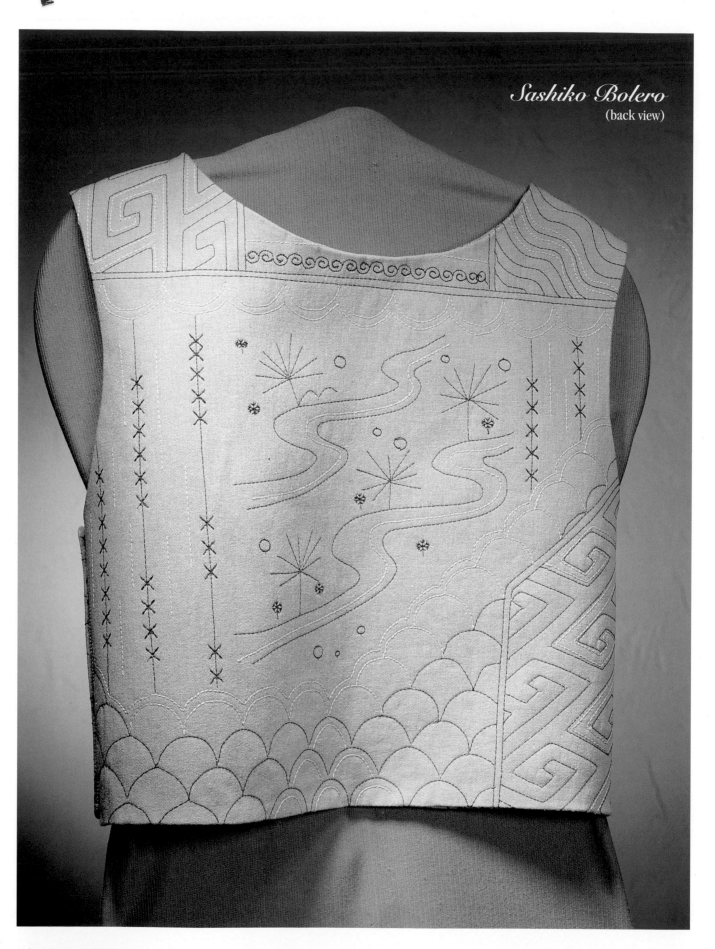

What Is Sashiko?

Sashiko is an ancient Japanese folk-art form of quilting, typically done with coarse white thread and long running stitches on dark, indigo-dyed, linenlike fabric. (To pronounce sashiko properly, rhyme "sash" with "posh" and stress the syllables evenly to say SASH-SHEE-KO.) Japanese folk garments were padded for warmth and durability, then embroidered with beautiful geometric patterns on the horizontal and vertical lines of the fabric's warp and weft—like designing on graph paper. There are hundreds of ancient patterns with special names and traditions. Many of them are familiar to western quilters today and are wonderfully adaptable to machine-stitching techniques. The three traditional patterns in "Sashiko Bolero" are Counterweights (the shape of weights used to measure gold), Lightning (dramatic angular lines), and Wave (known to western quilters as Clamshell).

Several areas are also embellished with built-in decorative machine stitches. The Japanese flower motif from a Pfaff embroidery card design is an excellent possibility.

You may have decorative patterns on your machine. These can be combined to produce interesting sashiko patterns. If your sewing machine has maxi-stitches, they can also be added to sashiko motifs. However, you can still create beautiful sashiko with a simple straight-stitch sewing machine.

Take a look around you and you will find traditional sashiko patterns in all kinds of unexpected but familiar places. Look at the patterns of your floor tiles, the roof of your house, the fence in your backyard, upholstered furniture, even your fabric stash. You will probably find traditional patterns woven or printed on some of them. Consult the books listed below. They show many traditional patterns and ways to draw and stitch them.

BOOKS ON MACHINE-STITCHED SASHIKO

Allen, Alice. *Sashiko Made Simple: Japanese Quilting by Machine*. Hinsdale, Ill.: Bernina Books Limited, 1992. Explains how to draw patterns on graph paper and how to find stitching routes.

Rostocki, Janet K. *Sashiko for Machine Stitching: Japanese-Style Quilting Classic to Contemporary*. Dayton, Ohio: Suma Design, 1988. Gives patterns for continuous-line quilting designs from nature.

Saunders, Jan. *ABC's of Machine Sashiko*. Communication Concepts (distributed by Madeira Marketing Ltd., Michigan City, Ind.), 1995.

BOOKS ON HAND-STITCHED SASHIKO

The following books have excellent graph diagrams and stories about traditional patterns. They are good references for finding patterns you can adapt to machine stitching. They are printed in English and are usually available in quilt shops.

Matsunaga, Karen Kim. *Japanese Country Quilting: Sashiko Patterns and Projects for Beginners*. Tokyo and New York: Kodansha International Ltd., 1990.

Otah, Kim, *Sashiko Quilting*. Seattle, Wash.: Kimi Ota, 1981.

_____. *The Classic Quilting of Sashiko*. Tokyo: Ondorisha Publishers, Ltd., 1990.

_____. *Sashiko: Traditional Japanese Quilt Designs*. Tokyo: Nihon Vogue Publishing Co., Ltd., 1989.

Takano, Saikoh. *Sashiko and Beyond: Techniques and Projects for Quilting in the Japanese Style*. Radnor, Pa.: Chilton Book Co., 1993.

Shopping List

Note: *A full-size bolero pattern appears on the pullout page. However, you can adapt these directions to other simple vests and jackets, using a garment pattern of your choice.*

¾ to 1¼ yds. each of denim*, lining fabric, and white or ivory lightweight fusible interfacing

Needle thread: 2 colors of cordonnet, Jeans Stitch, or topstitching thread

Bobbin thread: Cotton or cotton/polyester thread to match bolero fabric

Rayon embroidery threads for built-in decorative stitches

½ yd. hook-and-loop fastener, such as Velcro

Large sheets of tracing paper

Felt-tip pen

Pencil and eraser

Clear plastic ruler

Water-soluble marking pens or chalk

Open-toe embroidery foot

Embroidery sewing-machine needle or other large-eyed needle

#8 blunt tapestry needle

Tweezers

Optional (for a padded garment): Flannel or thin batting and lightweight, paper-backed fusible web

Optional: Baby powder, cornstarch, or cinnamon in a "pounce bag" (see page 35)

Optional: Enamel cloisonné pin

---

* Other good fabric choices for the bolero include linen and raw silk. Do not use black interfacing or you won't be able to see your threads when tying them off.

Cutting and Marking

Note: *Use the patterns on the pullout page.*

1. Trace the bolero pattern pieces and the sashiko patterns onto tracing paper. (For other garment patterns, you will need to plan the layout of the sashiko patterns, or use other sashiko patterns from one of the resources listed on page 33.)
2. Using the pattern, cut the bolero front and back from the denim, lining fabric, and fusible interfacing.
3. Fuse the interfacing to the wrong side of the bolero front and back to stabilize and prevent puckering while stitching the sashiko designs. The stabilized side will ride over the feed dogs to ensure smooth, even stitching. If you are using a flannel or batting layer in your bolero, use lightweight, paper-backed fusible web to fuse the flannel to the wrong side of the bolero front and back, then fuse the interfacing to the flannel or batting layer.

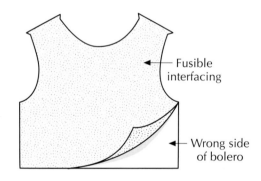

Fusible interfacing

Wrong side of bolero

4. Using fabric leftovers, make a practice piece of the same layers you will actually quilt for your bolero.
5. Choose a folk-art motif from those on the pullout page to use in place of the cloisonné pin. Trace the motif onto a separate piece of tracing paper and pin it in place on the bolero front pattern piece. If necessary, add to or eliminate some of the sashiko stitching around it.

6. With a pencil, lightly mark straight lines on your pattern where you want to do rows of decorative machine stitching (built-in stitch patterns) or a combination of straight and zigzag stitches. You can decide just which stitches to use later—after you have stitched some of the traditional patterns and learned the technique of sewing sashiko. Refer to the diagram below and the bolero photo for ideas. Depending on your machine, you may be able to create some of your own stitch patterns.

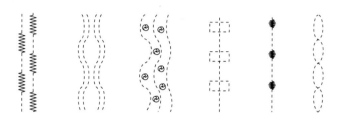

Easy decorative lines with mostly straight stitches

7. Mark the sashiko patterns on the right side of the bolero front and back pieces, using one of the following methods.

Puncture and pounce. This is a time-proven technique for transferring markings to fabric, but requires several go-rounds on the pattern.

Put an old unthreaded needle in the sewing machine, remove the bobbin, and lower or cover the feed dogs. Attach the open-toe foot and free-motion stitch the entire design on the paper pattern to puncture the design. Use a basting-length stitch to prevent the pattern from ripping.

To make a "pounce bag," put about 2 tablespoons of cornstarch or baby powder in the middle of an 8" square of muslin. Draw the corners together and wrap with thread or a rubber band to secure. If your fabric is white or light-colored, use cinnamon instead.

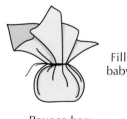

Fill with 2 tablespoons of baby powder or cinnamon.

Pounce bag

Place the punctured pattern on top of the bolero pieces and gently "pounce" the bag on the pattern along the perforations to lightly mark the design on the fabric. Check to see if it is transferring through the paper. Remove the paper and trace over the dots with a chalk pencil or water-soluble marking pen.

Use washable carbon tracing paper. It's available in several colors. Transfer the pattern, using a tracing wheel or a ballpoint pen. (Follow the manufacturer's instructions for removing marks when you have completed the bolero.)

Pin and stitch. If you would rather not mark the designs directly on the fabric, pin the tracing-paper pattern to the right side of the bolero piece and stitch through the pattern. You will have to remove the pattern pieces when you finish the stitching. Use tweezers to remove stubborn bits of paper from the stitches.

Doing the Sashiko Stitching

Creating the look of sashiko by machine requires special threading and tension adjustments.

1. Fill the bobbin with cotton or cotton/polyester thread that matches the bolero fabric.
2. Thread the needle with your main-color heavy thread, preferably cordonnet. (Cordonnet is slightly heavier than the other threads and imitates the hand-stitched cotton threads of traditional sashiko.) You can use the lighter-weight threads to vary the texture and color accents. If you are feeling especially creative, use 2 rayon threads in the needle. A touch of metallic or neon-colored thread can be fun too.
3. Tighten the needle tension almost as high as it will go. This causes the bobbin thread to come to the top, which creates the traditional space between the stitches. (That is why your bobbin thread must be the same color as the bolero fabric.)

Top thread
Bobbin thread

4. Set the stitch length at about 3.5mm (8 stitches per inch)—slightly longer than normal stitch length. Test your settings with several rows of stitching until it looks right and feeds properly.

5. Stitch the parallel lines that divide the pattern areas. If you are sewing on top of the tracing paper instead of following markings, remove the paper pattern temporarily, draw the lines with a chalk pencil or water-soluble marking pen, and then stitch on the lines. Replace the pattern. Stitch all dividing lines to define the pattern areas you will be sewing next.

6. Before you begin stitching the sashiko patterns, trace each pattern with your finger to find the longest route you can stitch before you run into another line that you do not want to cross. This is just like finding your way in a maze when you come to a "dead-end." You will

have starts and stops where you will have to tie off the threads and then move to another area to start. Be sure to stop *exactly* at the intersection. Read through the following tips before you stitch.

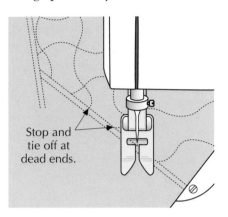

Stop and tie off at dead ends.

Sashiko Stitching Tips

- The folk-art motifs for the shoulder are continuous-line patterns. This means that you can start at one point and sew the entire pattern without stopping. Starting points are suggested on the pattern sketches.

- Always hold on to the thread tails as you begin sewing so the sashiko threads on top are not pulled to the underside in a big bunch. When turning corners or making tight curves, stop to pivot with the needle down, or engage the needle-down position if your machine has one. This results in nice square corners for precise sashiko stitching.

- If necessary, hold the fabric (so it doesn't feed as fast) to take the last complete stitch along a line.

- You may need to count stitches to ensure regular squares, such as in the Lightning pattern.

- When patterns go from one edge of the fabric to the other, you can stitch in the seam allowance to reach the next row of stitching so you don't have to cut the threads.

- When stops and starts are close together, raise the presser foot, draw the fabric to the back behind the presser foot to allow at least a 6"-long tail, and then lower the needle at the next starting point. You can cut the threads and tie off later.

- When you reach a line that you do not want to cross—a dead end—stop sewing and tie off, leaving 3"-long thread tails. Before you start stitching again, pull the top thread tail to the wrong side and tie off with the bobbin thread in a square knot. Use the tapestry needle to help pull the thread to the underside. Be sure the knot is tight before trimming the thread tails to about ½".

Tie in a square knot.

- Change colors or add other embellishments if you wish. If you add built-in stitches to your design, test them on practice fabric first for the correct tension setting and the threads best suited for the stitch. Cordonnet threads and topstitching threads are too heavy for most built-in stitches, but rayon thread is a good choice. Be sure to reset the tension to the high point when you return to the sashiko stitch.

You will be surprised to see how quickly your sashiko comes to life! Have fun sewing sashiko and stay on the lookout for traditional patterns. Once you have learned to "see" sashiko, you will discover patterns in surprising places.

Assembling and Finishing the Bolero

Note: *All seam allowances are ½" wide.*

1. On the wrong side of the bolero front and back pieces, mark each shoulder-seam intersection with a dot.
2. With right sides together, stitch the lining to the front and back bolero pieces, leaving a 4"- to 5"-long opening at the bottom edge. Begin or end stitching at the shoulder dots as shown, backstitching to secure each section.

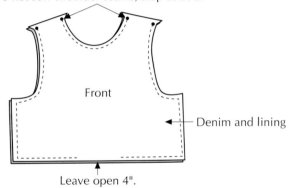

Do not sew shoulder seams; stop at dots.

Front

Denim and lining

Leave open 4".

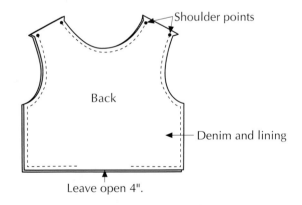

Shoulder points

Back

Denim and lining

Leave open 4".

3. Trim the seam allowances to ¼"; clip the curves and corners. Turn right side out and press carefully, making sure the lining rolls to the inside of the garment and doesn't peek out at the finished edges.

4. With right sides together, stitch the shoulder seams, keeping the lining free from the stitching.

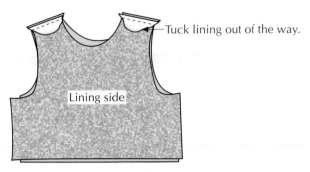

Tuck lining out of the way.

Lining side

5. To join the lining seams at the shoulder, turn under the raw edge of one seam allowance and slipstitch it to the remaining seam allowance at each shoulder. (If you prefer, you can reach inside the bolero through the lower opening, place the lining shoulder seams together, and stitch by machine.)

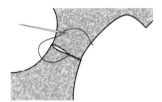

Slipstitch lining shoulder seams together.

6. Slipstitch the bottom openings closed on the bolero front and back.
7. Cut a piece of hook-and-loop fastener for each side-seam opening and stitch the hook portion of each piece to the right side of the back. Stitch the loop portion to the lining side of the front, using thread to match the bolero fabric in the bobbin.

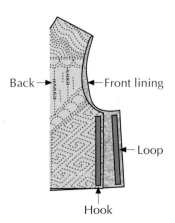

Back

Front lining

Loop

Hook

8. Press carefully, and your Sashiko Bolero is completed and ready to wear over a favorite blouse.

Woven Puzzle Vest

BY LOIS ERICSON

Hand-painted cotton, interwoven with a printed cotton that has lots of pattern movement, creates an interesting effect in this "handwoven" puzzle vest. A layer of black organza on top softens the contrast for a more subtle look, and a double layer of organza over the puzzle-fabric collar gives it a moiré touch. The corded closure and antique button add eye appeal, making this vest sophisticated enough for work, and elegant enough for a theater date. The idea for the woven-puzzle technique came from Lois's childhood, when her Swedish mother used woven paper strips to make Christmas tree ornaments. Lois simply transferred the idea to fabric and shaped the strips instead of using straight ones for additional intrigue and eye appeal.

Meet Lois Ericson

Lois Ericson has been manipulating fabrics and creating texture from ordinary cloth for twenty-five years. A self-taught fiber-art designer, she started writing books in 1969 because she wanted to share her information and her work with others who loved fabric, fiber, and fasteners. The path she chose led to teaching workshops, another activity she enjoys immensely. "I don't have one piece of paper that says I know how to do anything! There are no academic letters behind my name. I just know that I can solve design problems and I enjoy translating design ideas into reality with fabric," says Lois.

"My Swedish heritage has had a positive effect on me. I have a strong work ethic, but I don't aim for perfection, although good craftsmanship is important to me. My work is often regarded as having a Japanese influence. I consider that a very high compliment for my efforts."

Lois is the author of fourteen sewing books. Unique closures are her trademark. A lifetime of collecting fasteners of every description—old and new, traditional and not—led to her most recent book, *Opening & Closing*, a fascinating look at a variety of fasteners and innovative closures. She has also written numerous magazine articles, appeared on television, and made a video. She adds new designs to her popular Design and Sew pattern line each fall and spring.

Lois lives in Salem, Oregon, with her husband, Lennart. She rents a 5½-room house for her studio—a wonderful space to work, "play," and daydream, with classical music in the background. She loves sitting by the window in an antique chair with a cup of tea while she does some hand sewing. "That," says Lois, "is definitely joy in the making!"

Selecting Puzzle Fabric

The woven-puzzle effect is created by cutting and weaving two fabrics together to make a new fabric. You can use this woven fabric to create an entire garment, as shown here, or you can use it only for certain garment sections, such as yokes, collars, and cuffs. When selecting fabrics, look for closely woven fabrics in light to medium weights with some body. My favorite is cotton because there are so many color and print choices, the fabric is a good weight, and it usually has a crisp hand. To add body to limp fabrics, apply spray starch and press. Other fabric options and combinations include the following:

- One solid-colored cotton fabric with one printed one.
- Two printed cottons. Do not choose two really busy prints because the woven results can be distracting.
- One cotton print and an organza or other sheer fabric. I prefer organza because it is crisp and easy to use. Polyester organza is more transparent and shinier than silk organza, which has a mattelike finish and is slightly more opaque.
- A smooth, shiny fabric, such as satin or chintz, and a print or solid of the same or similar color but with an entirely different texture.
- Two menswear suiting fabrics. Wool worsted and serge are lightweight, smooth, and flat—perfect for weaving a more subtle fabric.
- Leather or synthetic suede, such as Ultra Suede. The edges won't ravel—a real plus if you decide not to use a sheer overlay on something like a handbag.

To make sure you like the results, make a small sample of the puzzle fabric with the two fabrics you've chosen.

If you decide to make yardage that you will cut into garment shapes later, work with only one yard of each fabric at a time (or only slightly longer than needed to accommodate the pattern piece). Larger pieces are more difficult to handle—at least until you are more experienced with the technique.

In addition to two fabrics for the woven vest, you will need sheer fabric to lay over each vest piece. The sheer fabric serves three purposes: it protects the unfinished edges of the woven strips, it can change the color of the fabric underneath, and it enhances the character of the new fabric you've created. You may want to wait to buy the sheer fabric until you've finished the weaving so you can take it to the fabric store to test sheer possibilities over it. Don't eliminate the idea of using a printed, textured, or metallic sheer overlay.

Examine the samples shown below and on the facing page to see how the character of the sheer can affect the results. Puzzle fabric can also be used without the sheer overlay but you will probably want to secure the cut edges using one of the methods shown in the sidebar on page 44.

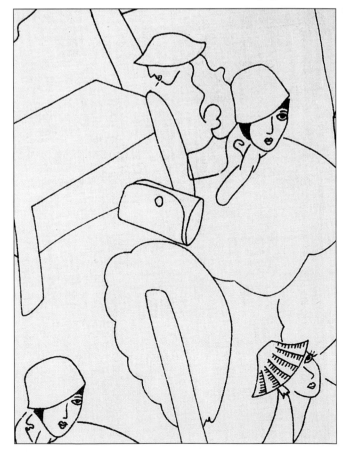

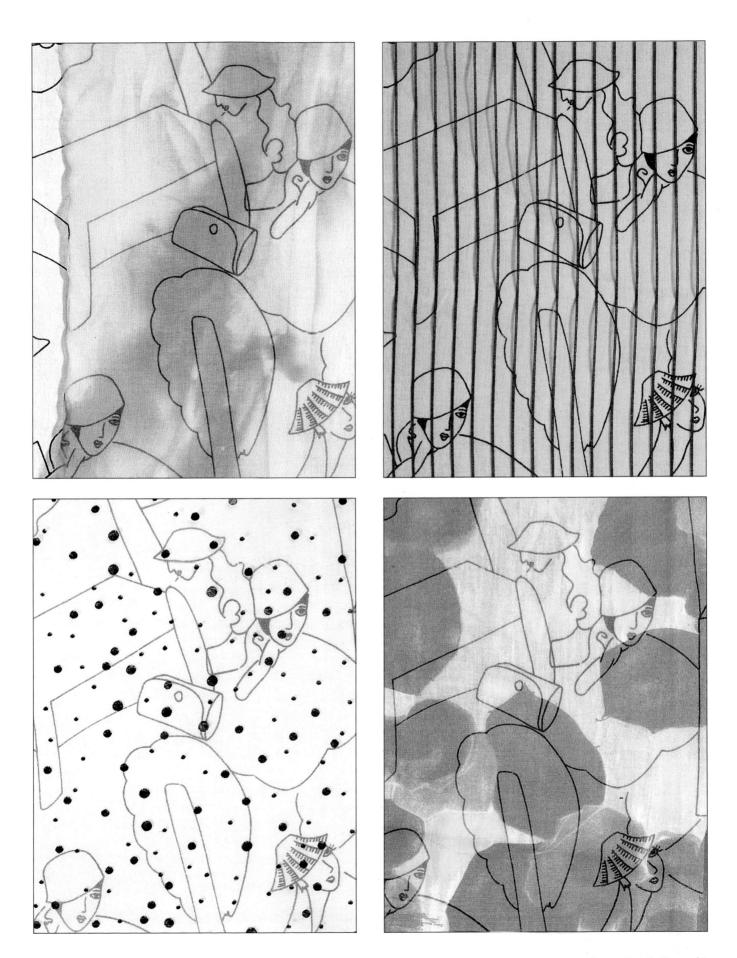

Shopping List

Note: *Refer to the pattern envelope for the required vest yardage when purchasing each fabric.*

Design and Sew Pattern #314*

2 contrasting or coordinating fabrics for weaving; refer to "Selecting Puzzle Fabric" on page 40

Lightweight fusible knit interfacing for 2 vest fronts and 1 vest back**

Lining fabric

Silk organza or other sheer fabric for top layer

Padded pressing surface or large piece of cardboard

2 yds. cotton cording for closure

Large, decorative button

* Look for this pattern at your local fabric/quilt shop or see page 95 for ordering information. You can use a similarly styled commercial vest pattern; however, you may need to adapt the pattern and adjust yardages.

**Double the recommended vest-pattern yardage if the interfacing is only 22" wide.

Cutting and Weaving the Puzzle Fabric

1. Cut 2 vest fronts and 1 vest back from *each* of the fabrics for the vest. You will have a total of 4 fronts and 2 complete backs. (If your pattern has a center back seam, you will have 4 back pieces, 2 for each back.) Cut 2 vest fronts and 1 vest back from the fusible interfacing and set aside until you have completed the puzzle weaving.

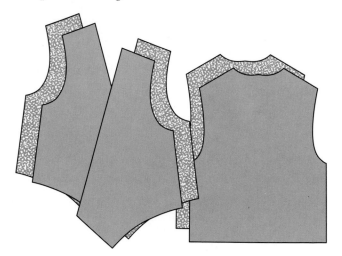

2. On the *wrong* side of 1 vest front only, make a series of vertical cuts the entire length of the piece. If you wish, you can draw the lines first. They can be straight, curved, or shaped as desired, and the number is up to you. The fewer the cuts, the larger the "puzzle pieces." Pin the pieces in order, *wrong side up*, on a padded pressing surface or a large piece of cardboard.

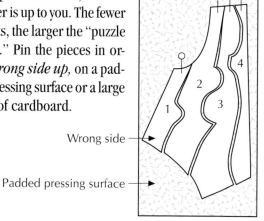

Wrong side

Padded pressing surface

3. On the *wrong* side of the companion piece for the same vest front, make a series of horizontal cuts, but do not cut all the way to the opposite edge. Leave at least ½" of each cut connected at the side seam until you are ready to weave, especially if you have made lots of cuts. It's important to keep the strips in order.

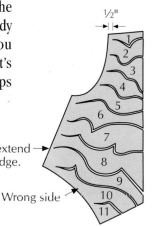

½"

Do not let cuts extend to side seam edge.

Wrong side

4. To begin weaving, cut the uppermost horizontal strip from the others and weave it across the vertical vest strips. Weave in a plain weave—over one, under one. Cut the next strip free and continue weaving, going over and under opposite strips from the first row. Continue in this alternating fashion until the entire vest front is woven, making sure that it is correctly shaped and that there are no open spaces between the rows in either direction. The pieces should fit together perfectly—just like a puzzle.

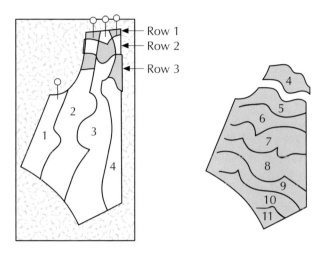

5. Trim ⅛" from all edges of the vest front interfacing. Place it face down on the wrong side of the completed woven front and fuse in place, following the manufacturer's directions. Pin the outer edges together to secure the sections that are not fused, then staystitch to keep them in place during handling.

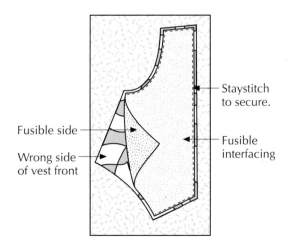

6. Complete the remaining vest front and back, following steps 1–5. Be sure to work with the wrong side up.

Designer TIP

To weave only part of a garment, such as a yoke:

1. Cut a paper pattern for the yoke. Place the garment piece wrong side up and mark the yoke line to indicate where to stop cutting. Make vertical cuts as desired, stopping each cut at the drawn line.

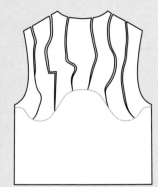

2. Place the yoke pattern on the wrong side of the remaining fabric for the horizontal weaving strips and cut out. Cut the yoke into horizontal strips.

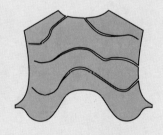

3. Begin weaving at the bottom of the yoke and end at the shoulder.

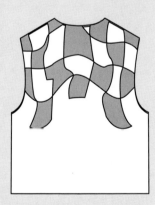

This technique also works for a woven bottom band—on sleeves, for example.

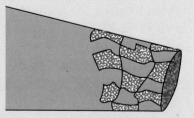

Try the puzzle technique for a sleeve band or the hem band on a skirt or long jacket.

For added design interest, consider the following:

- Do random straight stitching on the woven vest pieces *before* adding the sheer layer or instead of adding a sheer layer.

- Use side-by-side rows of straight stitching to outline each cut row. Try a contrasting color for more emphasis.

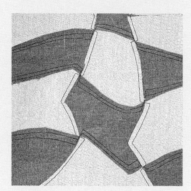

- Use a patterned machine stitch to outline the woven edges. Be sure to use a stitch wide enough to catch both raw edges.

- Position the sheer layer on top of the woven pieces, then stitch randomly or follow the woven pattern. Use straight satin stitching as shown or another decorative stitch.

Finishing the Vest

Note: *If you decide not to cover the woven pieces with a sheer fabric, you may want to do some decorative stitching as suggested in the "Designer Tip" above.*

1. Cut 2 vest fronts and the vest back (or backs) from the sheer fabric.
2. Position the sheer vest pieces right side up on the right side of each woven piece. Pin in place, then machine stitch ½" from the raw edges. Add more stitching if desired.
3. Assemble and line the vest, following the pattern directions. In the vest shown, the collars were covered with 2 layers of organza and finished with piping made from bias strips of one of the fabrics. If your pattern doesn't include a collar, you can design your own to catch in the vest front seam.
4. To duplicate the corded closure, cover a length of cording of the desired diameter with bias-cut strips of one of the vest fabrics as shown in the sidebar on the facing page. Make a separate piece of cording for each vest front, making them each 8" to 10" longer than the length of the front edge.
5. For the left front, finish one end of the covered cording by turning the edges in and hand tacking in place. If necessary, cut a bit of the cording away to make it easier to finish the end. Slip the button shank over the cording, then tie a loose knot. Position the button as

desired, then tack the cording to the vest front, just to the right of the button. On the other side of the button, tie a knot and stitch it to the vest.

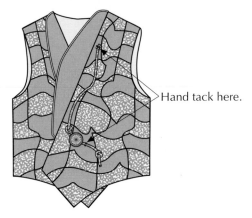

Hand tack here.

6. Arrange the remaining length of the cording loosely under the collar to determine how long to cut it. Cut it ¾" longer than desired. Push the fabric down so you can cut away ¾" of the cording. Turn under ⅜" at the raw end, secure with a few stitches, then wrap with

thread and end with a few stitches in place. Tack the cording to the vest.

Turn end under and wrap with thread.

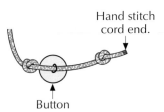

Hand stitch cord end.

Button

7. Finish one end of the remaining cording as you did the first piece. Make a loop at one end, large enough to accommodate the button and a knot at the end. Stitch and wrap the cording together on each side of the button opening. Knot the end.

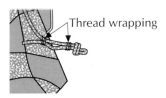

Thread wrapping

8. Finish and attach the remaining end under the collar as described for the cording on the left vest front.

Designer TIP

To cover cording:

1. Cut bias strips wide enough to wrap around the desired cording plus 2 seam allowances. Join bias strips as needed to make a piece the desired finished length plus 3".

2 seam allowances

Cut strips wide enough to encase cording.

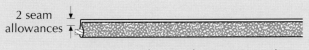

Piece strips at a 45° angle and press seams open.

2. Without cutting the cord, measure a length of cord equal to the length of the bias strip. Mark the length with a pin. Beginning at the pin, wrap the bias strip around the cord with right sides together. Stitch across the end, then stitch close to the cord, using a zipper foot or cording foot and taking care not to catch the cord in the stitches.

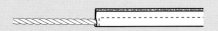

3. Slide the bias back onto the uncovered length of cord and trim the excess cord.

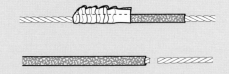

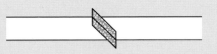

Irma's Stripes

BY MARY MASHUTA

Mary used ten Dutch fabrics to piece this stunning jacket. Each block is made of three matching striped triangles sewn to a triangular origami biscuit puff. You can use as few as two or as many as ten different striped fabrics to make your own version of Mary's jacket. Visually, you need to distinguish between the individual blocks, which you can accomplish with two alternating colors.

The allover pieced design was created with 6" equilateral triangle blocks arranged in an alternating pattern of red and purple. The striped fabrics in the collar band and the mock sleeve and hem bands were difficult to work into the triangular piecing for the larger garment pieces, but they added visual contrast and design interest. You can use other geometric pieced blocks in place of the triangles if you wish.

Meet Mary Mashuta

Mary Mashuta made her first wearables in the 1970s, five years after she took up quiltmaking. At the time, making wearables was less time-consuming than stitching quilts, but that is no longer true since she began sewing more elaborate ensembles. She has created eight outfits for the acclaimed Fairfield Fashion Show and four for the American Quilter's Society Fashion Show.

Mary first used stripes when creating garments for her book, *Wearable Art for Real People*. Intrigued by the design complexity and eye appeal that stripes add to simple blocks,

she applied what she had learned to creating quilts for her latest book, *Stripes in Quilts*. Mary loves the sophistication that allover designs give to wearables, and she enjoys discovering and developing the pieced blocks that, when joined, make these designs.

Mary is the author of one other quiltmaking book, *Story Quilts: Telling Your Tale in Fabric*. She is also a professionally trained teacher who has taught in more than half of the states and in Canada and South Africa. She lives in Berkeley, California.

Project Planning and Preparation

To make "Irma's Stripes," Mary used an equilateral 6" x 6" x 6" Origami Triangle block. You may wish to use an entirely different geometric block for your garment. When determining a possible block size for your garment, consider the scale of the block in relation to the garment pattern pieces. Will it fit comfortably into the pieces? Will the block be repeated often enough to be recognizable as a unit? Does the intended fabric show well in the size the block pieces will be cut?

Keep the shape and size of the desired block (or blocks) in mind as you look for a pattern, and be prepared to adjust the block size slightly to make it work within the pattern pieces of the garment. Adjusting it up or down by ¼" can make a big difference in how the block works.

Each 6" x 6" x 6" Origami Triangle block requires three 3" equilateral triangles cut from the same striped fabric, plus an origami biscuit puff of the same finished size for the center.

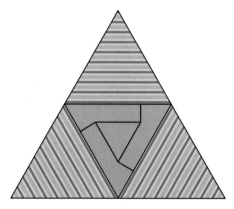

Origami Triangle Block

Geometric blocks work well in a jacket or vest with a straight bottom edge and simple design lines. Avoid darts if possible because they provide design challenges. (For more about darts and piecing, read through the directions for "Check It Out" on pages 87–95). Look for designs with simple band collars like the one shown instead of those requiring more complex construction. Remember, you can square off corners on patterns with rounded edges to make them more appropriate for geometric blocks. Avoid designs with overlapping. buttoned fronts, since planning for pieced design continuity is more difficult.

Change rounded edges to straight lines for geometric blocks.

Planning the block placement is a bit easier if the front and back pieces are about the same size. The kimono jacket pictured (PAW Prints #007 by Dana Bontrager) is a simple shape that is perfect for piecework. Look through commercial pattern books or through your stash of favorite patterns for other garment options.

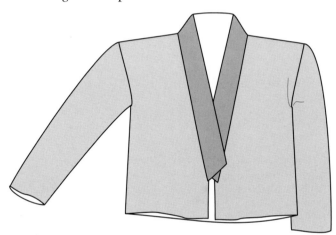

TIP Designer

To simplify a garment piecing project, consider the following options:
- Make a vest instead of a jacket.
- Use a striped or printed fabric instead of piecing jacket sleeves.
- Use plain fabric for collars, cuffs, and bands instead of piecing these.

Simple vest or jacket pattern, such as PAW Prints #007 by Dana Bontrager*

Red solid fabric for origami puffs in Origami Triangle blocks; use a single red fabric or several different ones

2 to 10 striped fabrics for blocks

Muslin to back Origami triangle blocks

Cotton flannel for batting in yardage recommended for jacket

Lining fabric in yardage recommended for jacket

Butcher paper

Template plastic

Transparent monofilament thread

Optional: Contrasting rayon embroidery thread for decorative machine quilting

Note: Supplies are listed for duplicating a jacket similar to the one shown. If you choose a different block design and/or pattern, you will need to adjust your shopping list. Read through "Determining Fabric Requirements" below.

* *Look for this pattern at your favorite fabric/quilt shop or see page 95 for ordering information.*

Determining Fabric Requirements

Use the template patterns on page 53.

1. Make any necessary adjustments for your figure; for example, add more room in the hips, if necessary, and lengthen or shorten the sleeve pattern as needed.

2. Measure the width and length of pattern pieces to determine if you need to scale down the chosen block size. If you're not sure, try positioning and tracing the block size and/or shape on the pattern pieces, using a pencil and ruler. Adjust the block size, if necessary, to better fit the garment pieces.

3. Make a sample garment if you wish. Cut it from muslin and baste together to be sure the size and style work well for you. Make any necessary adjustments for a good fit, and transfer them to the pattern. Yes, making a muslin sample takes a little time, but then you know for sure that you and the pattern are compatible before you spend all those hours piecing! Of course, one way to avoid this step is to choose a pattern you've already used.

4. Draw the adjusted pattern pieces on the uncoated side of butcher paper. Draw in the block placement. This is an optional step, but it is worth the extra time because it will help you visualize and finalize your project before you start cutting and piecing the blocks. It also makes it easier to calculate the number of whole and partial blocks you'll need to piece to fill up your pattern pieces, and is a handy reference when you are

arranging and sewing the blocks together to create the new "fabric" for each garment piece.

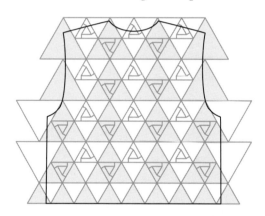

5. Count the number of triangles needed for your jacket. For the short kimono jacket shown (size medium), 440 striped triangles were used—214 red and 226 purple. These totals include the triangles for the collar, sleeve, and bottom bands. The actual number of triangles will vary, depending on the pattern you have selected, the pattern size, and the number of fabrics you use. Don't forget to count the number of triangle puffs you'll need. If a seam line cuts across one of these, and the resulting triangle is less than ¾ of a full-size triangle, don't plan to make an origami puff for it. Instead, cut a simple solid-colored triangle for that location, using the smaller triangle template provided. For my jacket, I needed a total of 82 red triangles, plus 82 muslin backing triangles for the origami puffs, and 24 plain triangles for those that ended up in partial blocks.

6. Trace the template pieces onto template plastic. Use the templates to determine how wide to cut fabric strips and how many triangles you can cut from a strip that is cut across the fabric width—approximately 42" to 44".

To cut the triangles for the origami puffs, you'll need to cut 4¼"-wide strips (to accommodate the height of the triangle template). You can cut approximately 15 triangles from each strip. Divide 15 into the total number required (82 for my jacket) to determine the number of strips required. Multiply by the strip width (4¼") to determine the minimum amount of fabric you will need for the puffs.

Repeat this process, using the smaller triangle template (requiring 3½"-wide strips) to determine how much more solid red fabric you'll need for the partial red triangles. You can cut about 19 of the smaller triangles from each strip. "Irma's Stripes" required a minimum of 32½" of fabric so I bought enough red fabrics to total 1 yard. Use the smaller triangle to also determine how much muslin to purchase—in this case, at least ½ yard.

Since stripes are generally printed or woven parallel to the selvage, and since you will be using more than one fabric, you will need to calculate the yardage based on cutting lengthwise strips rather than crosswise ones from each fabric. It's probably easier to estimate this, then buy extra to be safe. Be sure to plan so that all 3 striped triangles in a finished triangle patch are cut from the same striped fabric and that they are cut so the stripes are all following the same pattern from base to tip. For example, you would use triangles 1, 3, and 5 together in a block (see diagram below), and 2, 4, and 6 together.

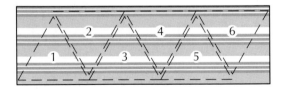

Uneven stripe

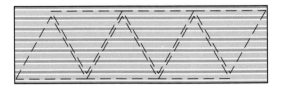

Even stripe

Cutting, Folding, and Piecing

1. Cut the required number of triangles from the striped fabrics, the red solid fabrics for the puffs, and the muslin for the puff backing.

2. To make an origami puff, mark midpoints on 3 sides of a muslin triangle by folding each side in half and creasing. Repeat with a red triangle.

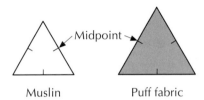

Muslin   Puff fabric

3. Place a red solid triangle on top of a muslin triangle and pin together at the upper right corner as shown. Place the pin perpendicular to the upper straight edge.

Match upper right corners.

4. Place a second perpendicular pin at the halfway point on one edge of the muslin triangle (even though it is not the true midpoint of the colored triangle on top of it). Pin through both layers.

Place second pin at muslin midpoint.

5. Pin the upper left corner of the red triangle to the corresponding corner of the muslin and press the excess fabric to the right. It will go beyond the midpoint of the muslin triangle underneath. Remove the second pin and reinsert it to hold both layers together.

Match upper left
corners and fold.

6. Rotate the triangle *clockwise* and repeat on the two remaining edges. Gently pat the folded triangle into place. Finger-press.

7. On the wrong side, hand tack the triangles together at each corner, using a double matching-color thread. Machine baste ⅛" from the raw edges. See the Designer Tip below.

Repeat with other two sides.
Machine baste ⅛" from edges.

8. Join 3 matching-stripe triangles to a biscuit puff to form each Origami Triangle block for your garment.

Step 1

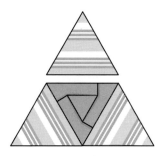

Step 2

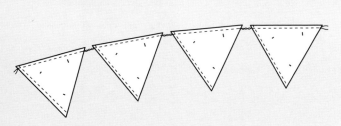

Step 3

Designer TIP

It is difficult to pivot at the corners on individual triangles when you are basting ⅛" from the edge. Instead, sew one edge of each triangle, chain fashion. After stitching one edge of each set of triangles, clip the threads between them and repeat the chain-stitching process for the next side. Repeat for the third side of each triangle. A single-stitch throat plate also makes stitching easier, since the hole the needle goes through is smaller and less apt to grab the fabric and pull it into the feed dogs.

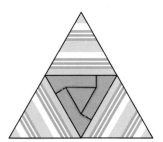

Chain stitch ⅛" from each edge of triangles.

9. Arrange the completed blocks in an alternating color pattern for each of the required pattern pieces, being careful to position the blocks without origami puffs at the edges. Stitch blocks together in a row, then join rows. Add bottom bands.

10. Position each pieced garment section on a corresponding flannel piece. Begin by lining up the triangular bands with the bottom edge.

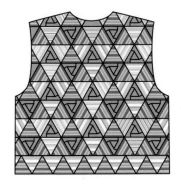

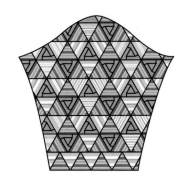

11. Use the small triangle template to cut enough triangles for the collar band. If the collar band is not the same finished width as the triangle, narrow or widen the pattern piece as needed. Sew the triangles together to the required length and cut to the required shape, using the collar band pattern piece. Cut a matching piece from lining fabric for the collar facing. Assemble and attach the collar, following the pattern directions.

Quilting and Assembling the Jacket

Many quilted garments are only quilted through the pieced "top" and the batting. The lining, added later, covers the batting and the underside of the quilting stitches. Machine quilting is the speediest way to quilt your pieced garment. "Irma's Stripes" was quilted to cotton flannel.

1. Safety-pin–baste each pieced garment section to a corresponding piece of flannel.

2. With transparent monofilament thread in the needle and regular thread in the bobbin, stitch in-the-ditch next to all seams, not just the major ones.

3. To add decorative machine quilting, machine stitch along the sides of each striped triangle with contrasting rayon embroidery thread in the needle. To show off the sheen of the thread, use a fairly long stitch (8 or 9 stitches per inch). Use the edge of your even-feed (walking foot) to make even-width quilting stitches on the triangles.

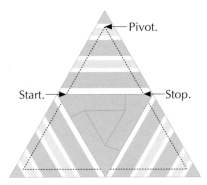

4. Assemble the garment and line it, following the pattern directions.

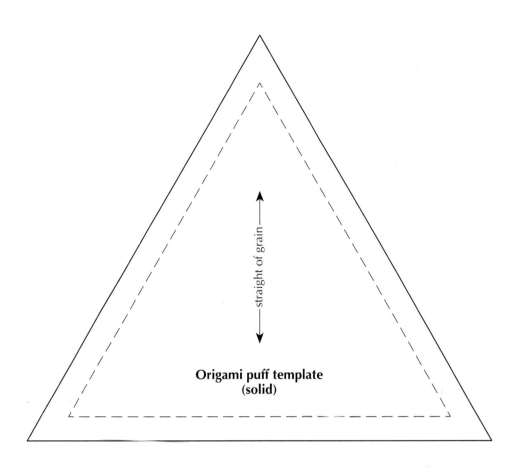

**Origami puff template
(solid)**

straight of grain

**Striped triangles and
muslin backing template**

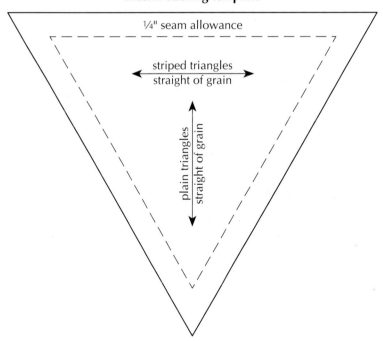

¼" seam allowance

striped triangles
straight of grain

plain triangles
straight of grain

A Penny for Your Stitches

BY JANET CARIJA BRANDT

Combine the beauty of Indian shisha-mirror embroidery with the ease of penny-rug appliqué and what do you get? An easy-to-make and fun-to-carry change purse. Real coins add glimmer to this little purse—three dimes, a nickel, and a penny. The coins are sandwiched under little discs of wool or felt, then appliquéd to the purse flaps. You might consider using penny sandwiches as appliqués on vests, jackets, and hats too. Substitute foreign coins if you have some wasting away in a drawer somewhere—what a great way to use them! Or use acrylic mirrors, available from your local craft store, to imitate real-glass shisha mirrors.

Meet
Janet Carija Brandt

One husband, two teenagers, two dogs, and one cat—plus lots of wool—share space with Janet Brandt in her Indianapolis, Indiana, home. Janet has been working with wool for many years. She uses it to sew, hook, knit, crochet, embroider, appliqué, and quilt. (She even sheltered a homeless, comical lamb named Leo one winter!) Janet has also designed a complete line of wool rug-hooking patterns as well as patterns for penny rugs and quilts. Her book,

WOW! Wool-on-Wool Folk Art Quilts (That Patchwork Place), features Janet's designs in bold, living color.

If you were to visit Janet, you'd find a project-in-progress in almost every room of her house. A state of creative clutter is ever present, and the language of "make-thing-itis" is well understood by all inhabitants. Her current focus is finding new ways to interpret designs in a wide variety of fabrics and techniques. That means she's making more things!

Shopping List

2 pieces of colorful wool (or other fabric), each 10" x 18", for purse
2 pieces of lining or cotton quilting fabric, each 10" x 18"
Prewashed wool or felt scraps in assorted colors for "pennies"
3 yds. narrow cording in a contrasting, coordinating color
Embroidery floss in assorted colors
Embroidery needle
Shiny pennies, nickels, dimes, or quarters
10" x 18" piece of pattern tracing paper
White glue or seam sealant

Cutting

Use the purse and penny pattern pieces on the pullout page.

Note: For this project, the term "penny" refers to the circular fabric shapes that enclose the coins.

1. Trace the purse pattern onto the tracing paper. Cut out and label one side "A" and the reverse side "B."

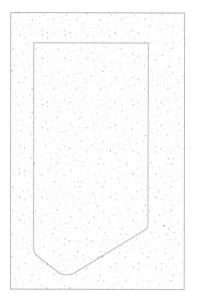

2. Pin the pattern to the right side of the purse fabric with the A side right side up. Cut out the shape. Repeat with the lining fabric. Flip the pattern to the B side and cut a purse shape from the remaining purse and lining fabrics.

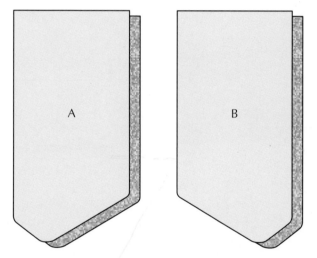

Cut 1 each from wool and from lining fabric.

3. From the wool scraps, cut decorative shapes for the pennies and dots in a variety of colors and sizes, using the patterns and referring to the photo. If you are using a woven fabric other than wool for the pennies, be sure to add ¼" all around each circle for a turn-under allowance when appliquéing. The decorative pennies are made of 3 layers: a coin captured between a fabric circle on the bottom and a doughnut shape on top.

Assembling the Purse

1. For each penny, thread 2 strands of embroidery floss into an embroidery needle and finish the inside circle of the doughnut shape with blanket stitches.

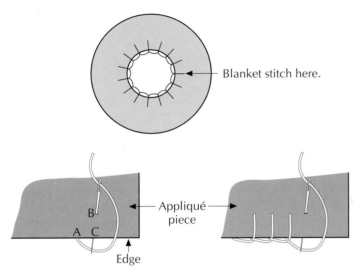

Blanket stitch here.

Appliqué piece

Edge

Blanket Stitch

2. Make a sandwich of the top penny, the desired coin, and a larger bottom penny.

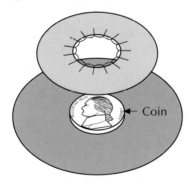

Coin

3. Stitch the outer edge of the top penny to the lower penny, using the blanket stitch and encasing the coin between the 2 layers.

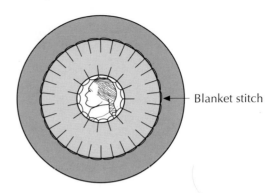

Blanket stitch

4. Complete all 5 penny stacks in this manner. Arrange the penny stacks and the small fabric dots on the right side of each purse piece, referring to the diagrams and photo. Be sure to position the pennies so that they won't get caught in the 1/4"-wide seam allowances.

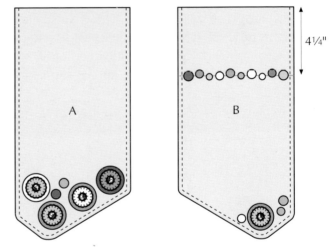

4 1/4"

A

B

Keep the appliqués away from the seam allowances.

When you are pleased with the arrangement, pin the penny stacks to the purse fabric. Temporarily fold the purse pieces into the final shape to make sure you are happy with the penny arrangement. Adjust as needed to fine-tune the color and placement. Attach the penny stacks to the purse fabric with blanket stitching.

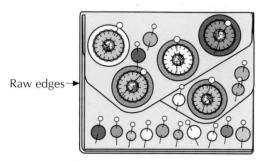

Raw edges→

5. With right sides together, stitch a lining piece to each purse piece, using a ¼"-wide seam allowance and leaving a 2"-long opening in one long side seam for turning. Backstitch at the beginning and end of the stitching. When you are within 1" of each corner and the point of the flap, change the stitch length to 20 stitches per inch. Stitch to the corner, pivot, stitch for 1", and then return to the normal stitch length. Clip the corners.

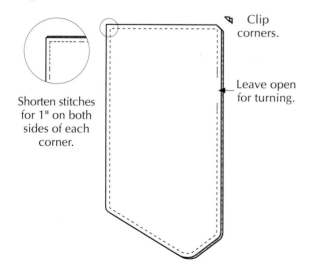

Clip corners.

Shorten stitches for 1" on both sides of each corner.

Leave open for turning.

6. Turn each piece right side out and press, using a steam iron and a press cloth. Slipstitch the opening edges closed, using closely spaced, invisible stitches.

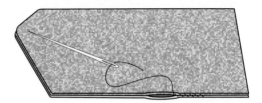

Slipstitch.

7. Fold each purse shape as shown, adjusting the flaps and folds to best show off the dots and pennies. Pin each purse along the side edges.

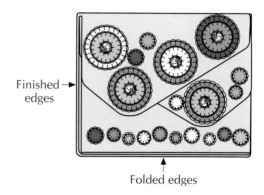

Finished → edges

Folded edges

8. Slipstitch the side edges of each purse together, then slipstitch the 2 purses together along the side and bottom edges.

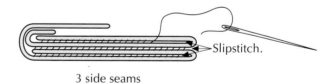

Slipstitch.

3 side seams

9. Fold the cording in half and tie the ends in a simple overhand knot, leaving a ½"-long tail. Treat the raw ends with a dab of white glue or seam sealant to prevent raveling.

10. Make a knot in the same manner every 3" along the length of the double cord. These knots add strength and decorative appeal as well as keep the cords from tangling.

3"

11. Tuck the ends of the cord into the upper corners of the top purse and hand tack securely in place.

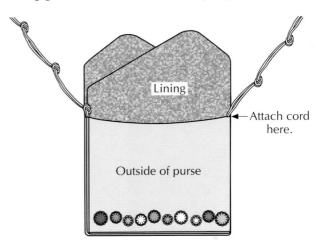

Lining

←Attach cord here.

Outside of purse

Elegant Tunic

BY MAGGIE WALKER

This reversible, midthigh-length tunic vest, with side slits for an easy fit, is embellished with appliqué and thread painting. It's the perfect showcase for hand-dyed or painted fabrics as well as all those gorgeous scraps and special-occasion or memory fabrics in your stash.

The method of construction differs from standard techniques, so be sure to read the directions carefully. You will create an elegant quilted side with Maggie's raw-edge appliqué, thread painting, and swirled-ribbon technique; then you'll make crazy patches for the reverse side. The resulting tunic is a soft, textured garment that doesn't cling, yet isn't stiff! It looks great with pants and a matching long-sleeved top.

Meet Maggie Walker

Maggie Walker has been using fabric as a medium of expression ever since she made a chance visit to the American Craft Museum in New York City nine years ago. At the time, she was representing several illustrators, including her husband, and doing freelance work as a graphic designer. As she walked by the museum on that working trip, Maggie spotted quilts from a contemporary quilt exhibit, and she was hooked. She began to collect fabric and make quilts. Joining quilt guilds and taking quilt classes was the natural next step.

As her fabric stash grew, Maggie began to dabble in experimental quiltmaking. Small collage and pieced wall quilts were soon followed by quilted clothing in which she used her own collage appliqué technique: composed arrangements of several different fabrics with attention to a natural cascading rhythm. She added swirling ribbons and threads over and under the appliqués, and the sewing machine became Maggie's drawing tool for thread painting, allowing her to visually weave the appliqués into the background fabric. As her technique gained exposure, Maggie was asked to teach art-to-wear classes. Developing garment patterns was a natural result of her sewing and teaching.

Maggie now hand dyes, paints, and scribbles on her fabric, so her quilts and garments are truly one-of-a-kind. She has had her work juried into regional and national arts-and-crafts shows. Sometimes Maggie's garments and quilts are the only fiber-art pieces in a show—coexisting with painting, sculpture, jewelry, and pottery. She was a finalist in the So-Fro House of Fabrics' America Contest, her work was juried into the prestigious American Quilter's Society Quilt Show in 1995, and several of her quilts have appeared in *Traditional Quiltworks* and *Quilting Today* magazines. Her reversible "Gypsy Vest" was featured in Sulky of America's *Patchwork Concepts in Sulky* and in *Sew News* magazine.

Elegant Tunic
by Maggie Walker
Everson, Pennsylvania, 1996.

Elegant Tunic detail

Elegant Tunic
Crazy-patched side reversed
(front and back views)

Shopping List

Vintage Vest pattern by Maggie Walker*

2½ yds. purple sueded rayon or a cotton print fabric that reads as a solid

2½ yds. muslin for foundation

Assorted floral-print fabrics with flowers and leaves in rich colors for appliqué collage

1 yd. violet-and-gold batik or other similar print fabric for bias binding

1 yd. black-and-gold print fabric for straight-of-grain piecing strips

1 yd. Japanese print in warm tones with a bit of red for side panels on crazy-patch side of vest

1 yd. small-scale black print fabric for folded strips on front of crazy-patch side

Scraps of assorted fabrics for crazy patching

Black thread

Purple rayon thread to match sueded rayon fabric for thread painting

Gold and pale violet rayon threads for random quilting on purple side of tunic**

Pale violet Ribbon Floss

Red rayon thread to embroider parts of crazy-patch side of tunic

¼"-wide red-violet satin ribbon to swirl down floral collage

Tracing paper

Freezer paper

Darning or quilting presser foot for free-motion stitching

Optional: Gluestick or pieces of fusible web

* Look for this pattern at your local fabric/quilt shop or see page 95 for ordering information. You can use a similarly styled commercial vest pattern; however, you may need to adapt the pattern and adjust yardages.

** Threads should contrast with the tunic fabric so the stitching is visible.

Preparation

1. Prewash all fabrics before you begin, unless you plan to dry-clean the finished tunic.

2. Trace the pattern pieces for your size onto tracing paper, tracing the *stitching lines* for the front, armhole, neckline, hem, and side-seam edges. At the shoulders, *trace the cutting line instead of the seam line.*

3. Cut out the new pattern pieces.

Making the Floral Collage Tunic Layer

1. Pin the pattern pieces to the muslin, allowing for an extra 1" all around each pattern piece, except at the center back fold. Cut out the pieces, eyeballing an extra 1" all around as you cut. It's not necessary to be exact.

2. Remove the pattern pieces from the muslin, then pin the muslin pieces to the wrong side of the purple rayon fabric and cut out along the cut edges of the muslin.

3. Pin and baste the fabric layers together for each piece, stitching 1" from all cut edges. Use plenty of pins in the body of the garment pieces to secure the two layers.

4. Place the muslin-backed rayon pieces on the floor with the purple fabric right side up so you can view them from a distance as you cut the

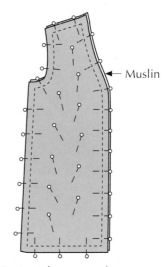

← Muslin

Baste 1" from raw edges.

appliqué pieces and plan their arrangement. Cut the desired pieces from the floral print. (I used larger flowers at the top of the tunic and began reducing the size as I cascaded the collage down the back. For the right front shoulder area, I cut medium to small flowers and leaves since the space for the collage is smaller.)

Work with the flower shapes on the back and right front to get a natural-looking arrangement. Don't worry if they seem to have too much contrast; the thread painting will modify the finished look of your composition. When you are finished cutting and arranging the flower components, walk away. Return to the pieces after a few hours for another look. Add, subtract, or rearrange flowers until you are satisfied with the design.

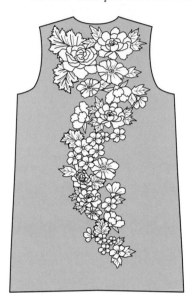

5. Swirl the red-violet satin ribbon over and under the pieces in the collage as desired. Tuck it under some pieces for a more integrated look. (Refer to the back view detail photo on page 63.)

6. Pin the flower shapes and ribbon in place, using plenty of pins to prevent them from shifting. You can anchor the collage edges with bits of fusible web or with gluestick; just don't use too much or the work will be stiff.

7. Thread the machine with purple rayon thread on top and in the bobbin. Begin the thread painting at the top of the tunic back and stitch from left to right, forward and back over the collage shapes only.

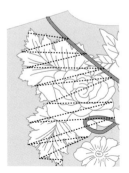

8. When you reach the bottom of the appliqué, set the stitch length to 0 and lower the feed dogs. Free-motion straight-stitch ¼" from the raw edges inside each appliqué piece.

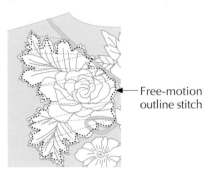

Free-motion outline stitch

9. Return the stitch length to 2.5mm and raise the feed dogs. Stitch over the appliqué in a different direction, to visually "weave" the composition into the background fabric.

10. Repeat steps 7–9 on the vest front.

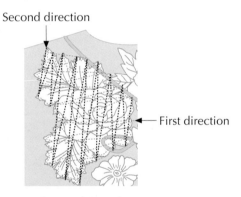

Second direction

First direction

Stitch over the appliqué in all directions to "paint" it evenly.

11. Fill the bobbin and the needle with gold rayon thread. Set the stitch length at 2.5mm. With the collage face up, begin stitching at the outer edge of the shoulder seam. Stitch down at an angle as shown, stopping at point A, opposite the center of the armhole. Stop with the needle down and pivot. Stitch to point B. Pivot and continue stitching to the remaining points as shown. Repeat with the remaining tunic front.

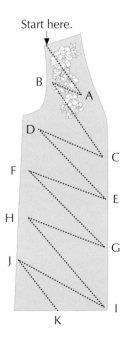

Start here.

8. Cut and sew a 1½"-wide black print strip to one side of each strip of crazy-patch blocks for the fronts. Cut 2 black print strips, each 1" wide, and fold in half lengthwise with wrong sides together. Press.

¾"

Fold and press strip.

Sew a folded strip to the remaining long edge of each patchwork strip for the fronts; stitch ¼" from the raw edges.

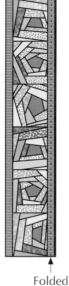

Folded strip

9. With right sides together, sew a strip of the pieced fabric to the edge of the patchwork with the folded strip. Press the seam toward the pieced strip.

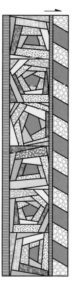

10. Center the crazy-patch blocks over the center crease on each tunic front and measure the uncovered space at the underarm. Cut 2 strips of Japanese fabric the length of the underarm measurement and add 1 strip to each edge of the black print strip as you did for the back panel.

11. Position a completed patchwork panel on each tunic front, centering as before. Pin securely in place. Turn the piece over and cut away any excess panel along the cut edges of the tunic front. Remove the crazy-patch side. You should now have 4 fronts and 2 backs for the vest.

Making the Shaped Binding

Use the pattern pieces on the pullout page and cut strips and pieces from the violet-and-gold batik print as directed below.

Note: *Bias-strip lengths are given for the Maggie Walker Vintage Vest pattern. If you are using a different pattern, you may need to adjust the lengths. Read through the directions carefully before you begin.*

1. Trace binding shapes onto freezer paper. Cut them out.
2. For the front-edge binding, cut 2 true-bias strips (45° angle), each 6" wide and the appropriate length (in chart below) for the size you are making.

Small	Medium	Large	Extra Large
19¼"	19¾"	20¼"	20¾"

Fold each strip in half lengthwise, wrong sides together, and press. With the straight edge along the fold, press the freezer-paper front-edge binding shape to the pressed binding strip. Cut out along the shaped edge. If necessary, carefully peel the freezer paper away and reposition along the remaining length of the pressed bias strip to continue cutting.

Folded edge of fabric strip

Freezer paper

3. Cut 1 bias strip, 6" x 20", for the shoulder appliqués. Fold in half lengthwise, wrong sides together, and press. Position the freezer-paper shoulder shape with the long edge on the fold and cut along the shaped edge. Remove the freezer paper, reposition, and cut the second shoulder piece.

Shoulder patches

4. Cut bias strips, each 2" x 24", for the side seams and set aside with the freezer-paper shape for the side strip.

5. From the remaining fabric, cut enough 3½"-wide, true-bias strips to total 7 yards. Sew the 3½"-wide bias strips together, short end to short end; press the seams open. Fold the resulting strip in half lengthwise, wrong sides together, and press.

   Cut the following pieces from the pressed bias strip for the size you are making.

Piece	Small	Medium	Large	Ex. Large
Neckline	14½"	15"	15½"	16"
Armhole, Hem, and Side Slit	5 yds.	5½ yds.	6 yds.	6½ yds.

6. Press the freezer-paper pattern for the neckline to the short bias strip, with the straight edge along the fold. Cut out along the shaped edges of the freezer-paper piece. Repeat with the remaining long piece of bias, removing the freezer paper and repositioning as needed to cut the entire piece.

Finishing the Tunic

1. Place the collage tunic pieces face down on a large, flat surface and smooth out to remove any wrinkles. Place the crazy-patch tunic pieces on top of the collage tunic pieces with wrong sides together. Smooth out any wrinkles and make sure the raw edges are even. Pin well at all raw edges and across the body of the tunic to hold the layers together. (Pins are not shown in the accompanying illustration.)

2. Thread the needle with purple rayon thread and the bobbin with red rayon thread. Set the stitch length at 2.5mm.

3. With the crazy-patch side of the layers right sides together, stitch the shoulder seams ½" from the raw edges. Trim the seam allowances to ¼" and press them open. You will cover the seams in the next step.

4. Center and pin a shoulder shape over each shoulder seam on the collage side of the tunic. To secure the shape and thread-paint the design, stitch across it from the armhole edge to the neckline edge and back, working from front to back.

5. To finish the armholes, wrap a shaped strip over the raw edges and pin, placing pins in the direction shown. Check the underside to make sure the bias is lying flat.

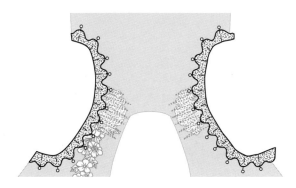

Adjust the sewing machine for free-motion stitching by changing the stitch length to 0 and lowering the feed dogs. Place the tunic under the needle with the collage side face up. Free-motion stitch the shaped bias with purple thread on the purple side and red thread on the crazy-patch side.

6. With right sides together, sew one short end of the right front shaped binding to the hem and side-slit shaped binding. Beginning at the pattern's positioning point for the button and loop, wrap the shaped bias over the raw edge of the right tunic front. Pin as you did for the armholes. When you reach the bottom edge, turn the corner, mitering it with an angled fold. Continue pinning in this fashion, mitering the corner as you wrap the side-seam-slit area. At the top of the slit, trim the bias at an angle as shown. Repeat with the left tunic front.

7. Pin shaped bias to the side-slit and bottom edges of the tunic back, mitering the corners and cutting the bias at an angle at the top of the slit as shown for the vest fronts.

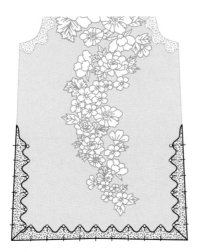

8. Fold the shaped bias for the neckline in half crosswise and mark the center with a pin. Beginning with the pin at the center back, wrap the shaped bias over the neckline edge. Pin carefully, easing the bias as needed to hug the curved edge. Continue down around the front neckline edges. When you reach the front bias, lap the neckline strips ½" over the center front shaped bias and trim away the excess. Turn under ¼" at each end of the neckline shaped bias strip and pin in place. Check the underside of the tunic to make sure the bias is lying smooth and wrinkle-free.

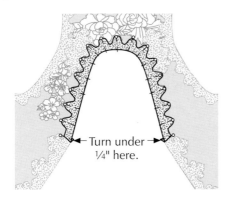

Turn under ¼" here.

9. With the machine still set for free-motion stitching, stitch the shaped strips to the tunic pieces as you did for the armholes. Begin stitching at the folded edge that joins the neckline strip to the center front strip. To end the stitching, take several stitches in place and clip the threads.

10. Adjust the sewing machine for a wide zigzag stitch (4mm or 5mm). With the crazy-patch side face up on the sewing machine, butt the front and back side-seam edges and zigzag together.

Zigzag edges together.

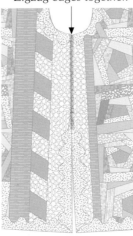

11. Using the freezer-paper pattern, cut the shaping for the side bias strips. Center and pin the shaped bias strip over the butted edges at each side seam, working on the crazy-patch side and starting at the slit. When you reach the armhole, wrap the strip over the edge to the other side and continue pinning in place, making sure the pins go through all layers. Remove the pins on the crazy-patch side.

12. Adjust the machine for a 2.5mm stitch length. With the feed dogs up, purple rayon thread in the needle, and red rayon thread in the bobbin, stitch forward and reverse lines across the shaped bias strip along the entire length of each side strip.

Pin. Stitch.

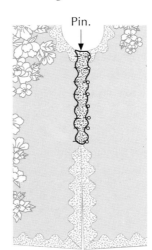
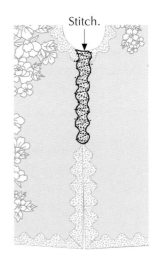

Love of Life, Love of Color

BY GRACE FRANCE

If you haven't experimented with pin weaving yet, here's your chance to try it for some free-spirited, creative fun. Adding colorful, pin-woven sleeves to a favorite vest turned it into a "vest jacket." Lots of embellishment—shisha mirrors, buttons, beads, charms, and jewels—add tactile and visual interest to the sleeves as well as to the vest fronts and back.

Meet Grace France

Until recently, Grace France was an associate professor of education at Montana State University in Bozeman. Now retired, Grace channels her creativity into designing and producing one-of-a-kind wearables. Her list of accomplishments and teaching credits are as broad as her vivid and creative imagination. She has won numerous awards for her work, and several of her garments have been featured in galleries and shows throughout the western United States.

Gifted with artistic ability and a wonderful sense of humor, Grace uses a wide range (and often surprising combination) of yarns, fibers, fabrics, textures, and embellishments in her colorful, always classy, and often entertaining contemporary clothing. The garment featured here is a typical example of her work; it includes wet-and-wrinkled fabric, a pleated panel, decorative stitching, and pin weaving—all

tastefully combined in a unique jacket vest. Wonderful embellishments, seen from a distance, enhance the bright colors. Up close, they amaze and amuse.

Grace's trademark, whether stitching or teaching, is removing boundaries and opening her students' minds to the freedom of playing with new techniques and materials. She guides her students to design and complete garments that are unique but very wearable.

Grace also adds "accomplished horsewoman" to her list of credits. Gaited horses—two Tennessee Walkers and a Missouri Fox Trotter—solved a potentially limiting back problem she has. Grace and her husband, Gary, both natives of Montana, live on a ranch surrounded by a herd of Texas longhorns, eleven cats, and three dogs!

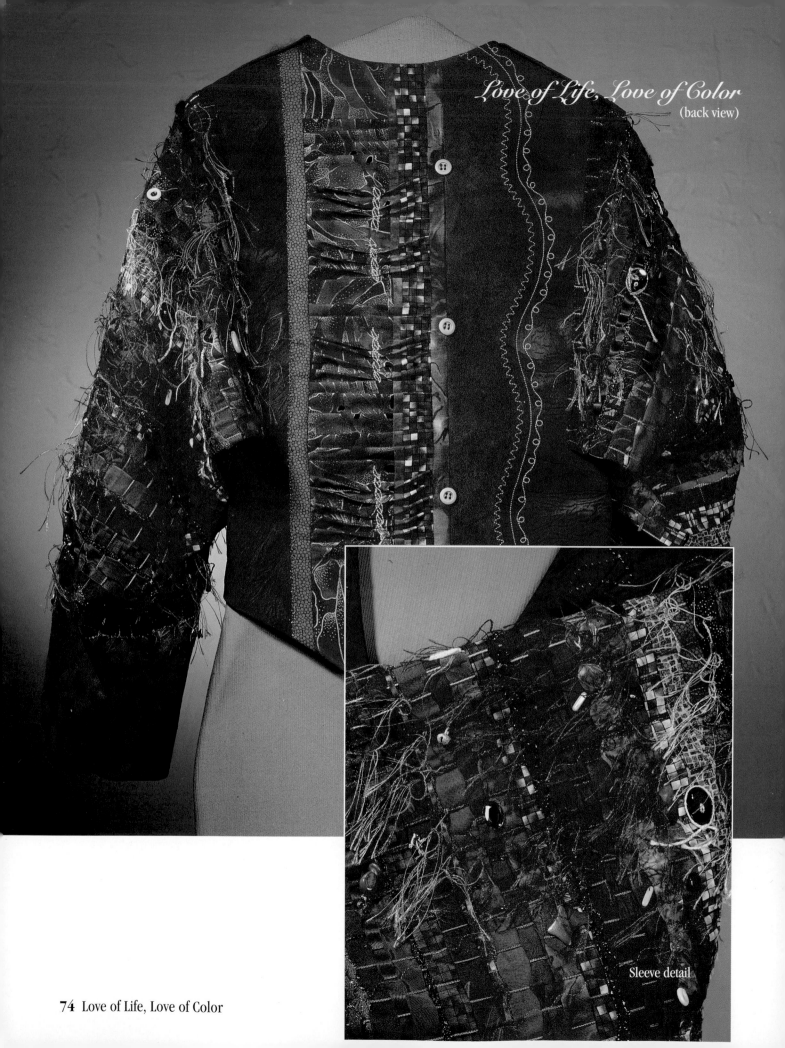

Sleeve detail

Shopping List

Commercial vest pattern of your choice
30" x 30" piece of pattern tracing cloth or tracing paper
Black marking pen
2 yds. of 45"-wide hand-dyed (or hand-dyed look-alike) solid for vest front and back
¾ yd. theme print fabric for sleeve bands, weaving strips, and pleated back strip
3 yds. of 45"-wide lightweight woven, weft insertion, or tricot knit fusible interfacing*
50 to 60 yds. of assorted ribbon, string, pearl cotton, or anything of similar weight for pin weaving
2 yds. or more each of several novelty yarns, bias tape, trim, and ribbon for pin weaving
1¼"-wide fabric strips (2 each of 15 to 20 colors) for pin-woven sleeves, to coordinate and contrast with theme print
Assorted embellishments: beads, buttons, shisha mirrors, semiprecious stones, plastic jewels, seashells, charms, etc.**
3 yds. of 45"-wide lining fabric
30" x 30" piece of cardboard for pin weaving
Long, glass-headed pins
Invisible thread

Optional Supplies
Large-eyed, blunt needle for weaving yarns and ribbons
Pleater for pleated back section
3" x 45" strip of synthetic suede, such as Ultra Suede, for jacket back
Lightweight fusible web to hold appliqué edges in place

* You will need 6 yds. if it is 28" wide or less.
** Keep your eyes open for embellishment treasures at thrift shops and garage sales, and in junk drawers and fishing-tackle boxes. Refer to the embellishing directions for additional ideas.

Preparation

1. At least one day before you begin the project, dampen the hand-dyed fabric, then twist it and tie it in a big knot. Use rubber bands to hold the shape if necessary. Allow to dry.

2. Following the diagram at right, draft the sleeve shape onto pattern tracing cloth or tracing paper. To determine how long to make the pattern, measure from a point 2" in from your shoulder edge to your wrist or wherever you want the sleeve to end. Cut out the pattern piece.

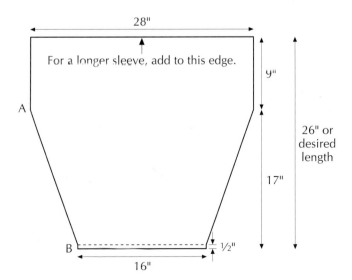

Pin Weaving the Sleeves

1. From the theme print fabric, cut 1 strip, 8½" wide, across the fabric width and set aside for the sleeve bands. Cut 1 strip, 4" wide, across the fabric width and reserve for the back pleated panel (optional). Cut a few 1¼"-wide strips from the remaining fabric to use in the pin weaving.

2. Cut 2 sleeves from the fusible interfacing.

3. Position 1 interfacing sleeve on the cardboard with the fusible side face up and pin in place at several locations. To create guides for the warp, place pins about ½" apart at a slant, away from the top edge of the interfacing. Place a row of pins through the interfacing and the cardboard, 8" from the sleeve bottom edge, making sure the pins are directly opposite the pins along the top of the sleeve as shown. You should have the same number of pins (total) as there are across the top.

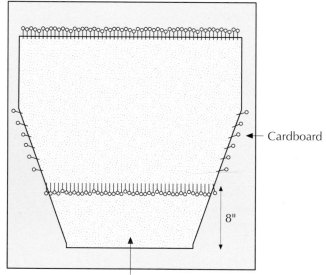

Cardboard

8"

Fusible side of interfacing

4. To warp your "loom," tie a slipknot at one end of the string or yarn, leaving a 1"-long loop. Slip the loop over the first pin at the upper left-hand corner of the sleeve, then wrap the warp thread down and around the first two pins at the bottom of the sleeve. Bring the thread back to the top of the sleeve, wrap it around the next two pins, then wrap it around the next two pins at the bottom. Continue wrapping the warp in this manner, until the entire sleeve loom is warped. When you reach the last pin, secure the yarn with a slipknot as you did at the beginning.

Note: *If you wish to change yarns when warping the loom, tie the new yarn to the other yarn with a secure square knot and leave the ends as embellishment.*

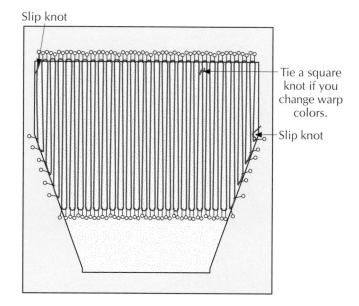

Slip knot

Tie a square knot if you change warp colors.

Slip knot

5. Before you begin to weave with the 1¼"-wide strips, decide whether you want a raw-edge, rag-rug look to the finished sleeve or a more finished appearance. If it is the latter, turn under and press ⅛" on *each* long edge of the strips, except for the ones you will use for the first and last row of weaving. Turn under and press only one edge (the bottom edge) on the first strip before you begin.

6. Beginning at the top of the sleeve, weave a 1¼"-wide strip over and under the warp, *catching it through the loop on the left-hand pin.* Push the strip up against the pins across the top. Add a second strip, reversing

the weaving so it goes over and under the opposite warp from the first row. Continue weaving in this manner in the desired color order, adding strips of yarn, bias tape, trim, and ribbon as desired for added texture and design interest. Use a blunt, large-eyed needle to make weaving ribbons and yarns easier. End the weaving with a 1¼"-wide strip of fabric (with the bottom edge turned under and pressed).

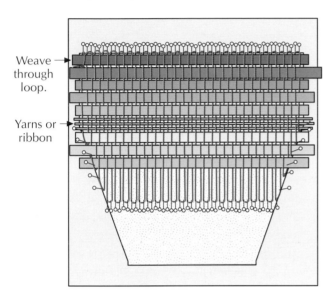

Weave through loop.

Yarns or ribbon

7. From the theme print fabric, cut 2 strips, each 8¼" wide, to fit the lower, unwoven section of the sleeves. Turn under ¼" at the top edge of each strip. Pin a strip to the sleeve, making sure it is wide enough to overlap the raw edge of the last weaving strip when the pins are removed. You will stitch it in place after fusing and removing the pins.

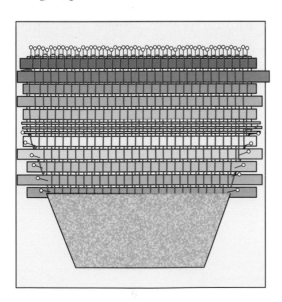

8. Place a press cloth over the completed weaving and steam press for a few seconds to set the weave.

9. Remove all pins and carefully turn the sleeve over on the ironing board. Steam press to fuse the weaving and the lower band of theme fabric to the interfacing.

10. Repeat steps 1–9 to complete the second sleeve. You don't need to duplicate the first sleeve. Feel free to vary the weaving pattern with the desired fabric and trim colors. Refer to the photograph for ideas.

11. Edgestitch along the top edge of the theme fabric at the lower edge of each sleeve. To further secure the pin-woven section, stitch through the strips with a straight or serpentine stitch in a random pattern. Use invisible thread in the needle and stitch the rows on the diagonal of the sleeve, spacing them about 2" apart.

12. Secure the outer edges of the pin weaving on each sleeve by straight stitching or zigzagging ¼" from the sleeve raw edges. With the edges secured, it will be easier to embellish the sleeves.

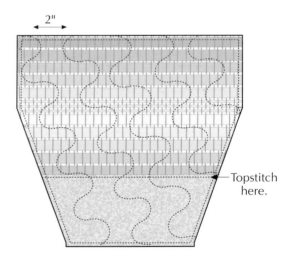

2"

Topstitch here.

"Quilt" the sleeves with straight or serpentine decorative stitching.

Creating the Garment Pieces

1. Cut the vest fronts and the back from the interfacing.
2. Pin one of the interfacing fronts to your ironing board with the fusible side face up.

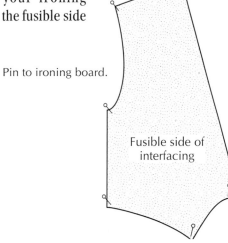

Pin to ironing board.

Fusible side of interfacing

3. Untie the *dry*, wrinkled fabric and place it on the interfacing, leaving as many or as few wrinkles in the fabric as you like. Make sure you leave a large-enough piece for the other front and the back. Use a few pins to secure it and trim away the excess. Fuse the wrinkled fabric to the interfacing. Repeat with the remaining front and the back. Trim the excess wrinkled fabric even with the edges of the interfacing, making sure both vest fronts are the same size and shape. Trim as needed.

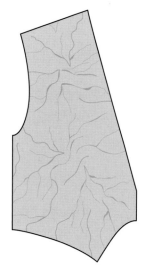

4. Using the vest pieces as your pattern, cut out 2 lining fronts and 1 lining back. Set aside until the embellishment is complete.
5. Referring to the photo on the facing page and the sidebar on embellishments on pages 80–81, embellish the sleeves to your heart's content, being careful to keep the embellishments a few inches away from the underarm seam allowances. (Why waste the "pretties" on the sleeve underarms where they won't be seen anyway?)

6. Fold one of the sleeves in half and place it on a vest front, with the straight edge the desired distance in from the shoulder. Use a few pins to outline the area the sleeve covers because you will not place any embellishment in that area. Repeat with the other vest front and the vest back.

Folded sleeve

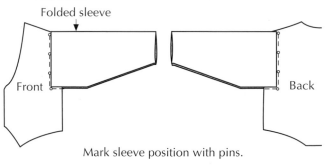

Front   Back

Mark sleeve position with pins.

7. With the vest fronts face up and side by side, arrange novelty yarns on each front to create a balanced design. Hand sew or machine couch the yarns in place. To machine couch, lower the feed dogs and remove the presser foot. Pin the yarns in the desired position and shape. Stitch several short stitches alongside the yarn to get started, then move the fabric with both hands so the needle will stitch over the yarn several times. Straight-stitch alongside the yarn for a few stitches and then over it. Repeat along the entire length of the yarn. You can also use transparent nylon or polyester thread in the needle and use a medium-length, narrow stitch to zigzag over the yarn.
8. Embellish the fronts with seed beads, sequins, buttons, etc., taking care to keep the design balanced. Your garment will be more interesting if the two fronts are *not* identical. For added embellishments, cut shapes from the theme fabric and fuse in place with fusible web. Fuse in place on the fronts and further embellish with beads to cover the raw edges.

(continued on page 82)

KEY

1. Shell beads sewn on four different ways
2. Metallic beads sewn on four different ways
3. Hanging beads with one large stone
4. Wooden bead tied on with silk ribbon
5. Metallic thread knotted into a bead
6. Bugle bead with seed bead on each end
7. Button tied on with bead in center
8. Plastic metallic disc and adhesive forms
9. Plastic net from grapes with seed beads in center
10. Stacked buttons (use larger ones for a decorative effect)
11. Plastic pockets with beads and sequin discs inside
12. Misc. sample of beads, buttons, etc., sewn on by machine

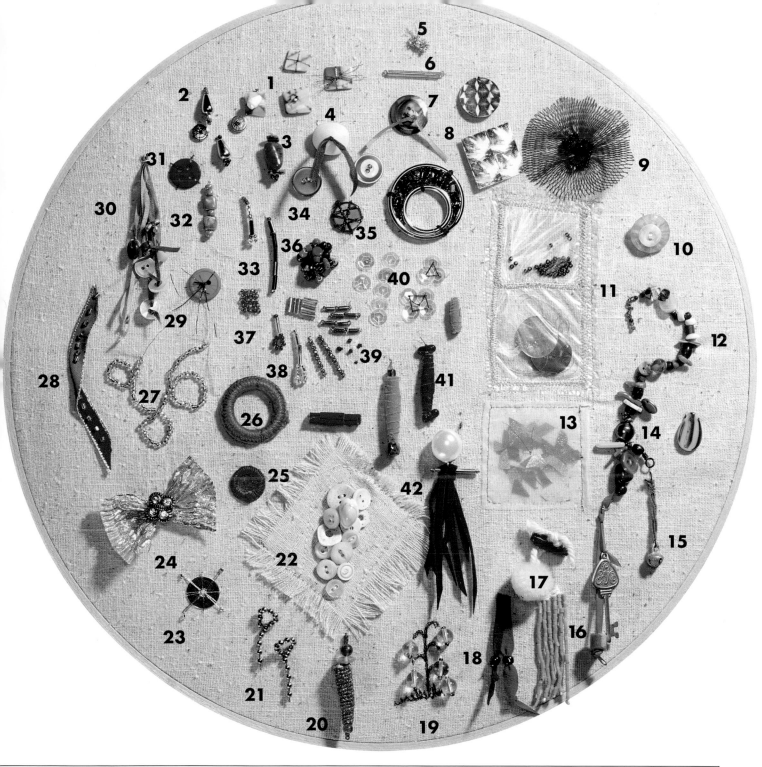

13. Sheer organza fabric with lamé chips inside pocket
14. Chenille from fishing supplies and hanging bell
15. Charm and bead hanging from silk ribbon
16. Commercial bead fringe
17. Cotton-ball fringe and button
18. Ultra Suede strip with bead knotted on
19. Bead flowers with machine-stitched stems
20. Floral wire zigzagged with metallic thread, shaped to a bead form
21. Chains cut off a small key chain
22. Antique buttons overlapped with a bone bead and shell
23. Washer sewn with metallic thread
24. Antique button sewn on gathered lamé
25. Commercial shisha mirror sewn on by hand
26. Covered brass ring (buttonhole stitch using pearl cotton thread)
27. Seed beads sewn on by machine

28. Seed beads sewn on double-sided ribbon
29. Button sewn on with metallic thread
30. Buttons and beads hanging from silk ribbon
31. Decorative button sewn on four sides
32. Hanging beads
33. Seed and bugle bead combination for a hanging fringe
34. Button with seed bead in center
35. Decorative button overlapped with metallic thread
36. Button made with overlapping beads of various sizes
37. Lazy daisy stitch with seed beads
38. Seed bead and bugle beads sewn on several ways
39. French knots made from thread
40. Sequins sewn on five different ways
41. Beads made from fabric, sewn stationary and left hanging
42. Found object made into fringe and bead combination

Embellishment Ideas

Designing with embellishments is a spontaneous, intuitive activity, and the results will depend on the range of items you have collected. Embellishments add a playful, whimsical effect to almost any garment. Examine the close-up of the jacket sleeves to see what I mean. My definition of embellishment is anything you can dangle or attach. Use as few or as many of the following ideas for embellishing as you wish.

Buttons: old or new, alone or in combination. Try stacking them or use them in clusters of two or more.

Fishing gear: fancy lures and flies. Be sure to dull the hook and remove the barb. Plastic worms are another great fishing-gear find!

Shells: natural for embellishment work. Look for them in bead and gem shops. Most shells and shell pieces have a small hole or two where you can take several stitches to secure them. Sew flat shells creatively, using metallic or other decorative thread.

Coins: those travel souvenirs you never seem to use. Leftover tokens work too. Some coins have holes, but you can also drill a small hole and attach the coin with heavy thread.

Junk-drawer delights: washers, cotter pins, small screws, bolts, springs, buckles, etc. Attach these with buttonhole twist or quilting thread.

Beads: from a jewelry box, garage sale, or thrift shop. Try changing undesirable colors with acrylic paints.

Charms: from existing necklaces and bracelets. New ones are widely available in fabric and craft shops. Try using dental floss to attach these. It's strong, but use a dab of fabric glue on the underside after knotting the floss for added security.

Chains (plastic or metal): from necklaces, bracelets, or key chains. These add wonderful movement when used on clothing.

Plastic jewels: readily available at craft and fabric shops. Also look for these on thrift-store clothing. Glue on if they don't have holes. Further embellish with yarn as shown.

Bells: to add movement and a little song. Christmas is a good time to find these. Check bead shops for ethnic-style bells too.

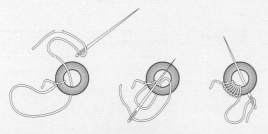

Shisha mirrors: a favorite source of "flash" on wearables. Look for small glass or acrylic mirrors in craft stores or mail-order catalogs. Attach as shown.

Place plastic ring over mirror and cover with thread.

Plastic netting: think produce department. You can make a rosette from the netting that comes around garlic or grape clusters for a colorful, inexpensive, and unusual touch.

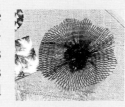

Floral wire shapes: the covered type from a floral shop or the floral department in your local craft shop. Satin-stitch zigzag over it on the machine (a piping or beading foot helps), then form it into round beads or wrap it around a pencil point for shaped beads.

Eyelash yarn or faux-fur yarn: tied on for added texture. Use a 6"-long piece and loop it around the warp.

Tuck a loop of eyelash yarn behind a warp thread.

Pull ends through loop and tug to tighten around warp.

Bead "buttons": can be decorative or functional. Sew a small wad of fabric to the garment, then cover it with beads. Thread a beading needle with nylon beading thread and place enough beads on the needle to cover the wad of fabric. Repeat until the wad is covered.

← Wad of fabric

Sew to foundation fabric.

Add a string of seed beads.

Add more strings of beads to cover the fabric wad.

(continued from page 78)

9. Embellish the back in a similar manner, or if you prefer, make a pleated back like the one pictured.

To make a pleated back: Cut the reserved 4"-wide strip of theme print fabric to equal twice the length of the vest back. Place the strip right side down on the pleater with 4" extending below the bottom edge of the pleater. Pleat the strip in any desired combination of pleating strategies. For example, you can get deeper pleats by skipping one or more louvers in the pleater. Vary the pleat spacing as desired, and make a strip that is equal to the length of the vest back, with the top 4" and the last 4" of the strip unpleated.

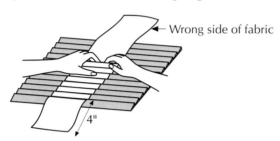

← Wrong side of fabric

4"

Cut a 4"-wide strip of fusible interfacing to match the length of the pleated strip. Place it, fusible side down, on top of the pleated strip (still in the pleater) and fuse it in place. Allow to cool, then remove the pleated strip from the pleater.

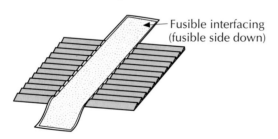

Fusible interfacing (fusible side down)

Sew a 1¼"-wide strip of fabric to each long edge of the pleated strip, using ¼"-wide seams. Press the seams toward the strips.

If you are using synthetic suede on the jacket back, cut one edge of the 3"-wide strip in an interesting curvy shape. If you prefer to use a woven fabric instead, cut a 3"-wide strip and cut curvy edges as well. Sew the strip to the right-hand edge of the strip-bordered pleated panel and press the seam toward the border strip. Turn under and press ¼" along the remaining border strip.

Position the completed back panel on the vest back and pin in place. Edgestitch in place, then use a decorative stitch, such as a blanket or serpentine stitch, in a contrasting thread to embellish the edges. If you used a woven fabric

instead of synthetic suede, you may want to satin-stitch over the raw edges. In that case, use narrow strips of fusible web to hold the edges in place for stitching.

For added texture, turn several of the pleats in the opposite direction and pin. Stitch across the center of the pleated strip, using a contrasting thread and a decorative stitch.

If desired, do additional decorative stitching to the right of the suede strip, being careful to keep the stitching out of the area where you will attach the sleeve.

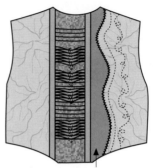

Shaped synthetic suede strip

Assembling the Jacket Vest

1. With right sides together, pin a lining piece to each completed vest front and back. Stitch around the back and each front piece, using the seam allowance called for in your pattern, except along the shoulder and side seams where you use ¼"-wide seam allowances. Leave a 4"-long opening in the side seam on each front and 1 side seam on the back. Turn each piece right side out through the opening in the seam and press, making sure the lining rolls to the underside at the finished edges. Slipstitch the opening edges together. If desired, topstitch each piece ¼" away from all finished edges.

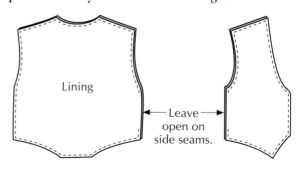

Lining

← Leave → open on side seams.

2. Pin the fronts to the backs, with the finished shoulder- and side-seam edges overlapping the back by ⅜" to ½". (Side seams only are shown in the illustration.) Try the vest on and adjust the fit as needed. Topstitch the pieces in place ¼" from the finished front shoulder and side front edges.

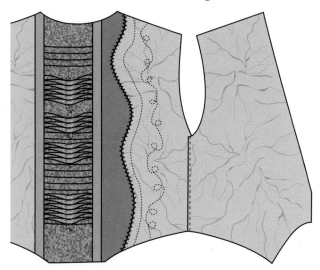

Lap fronts over back at side seams.
Topstitch ¼" from edge. Repeat with shoulder seams.

3. With right sides together, pin a lining piece to each completed sleeve. Stitch ½" from the lower edge and ½" from the upper side and top edges (from point A to the opposite point A) of each sleeve. Leave each long edge open between points A and B. Trim the seams to ¼". Turn right side out and press.

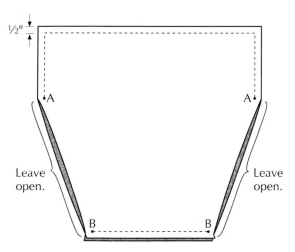

4. With the sleeves right sides together, stitch ⅝" from the raw edges of the sleeve between points A and B, *keeping the lining free from the stitching.*

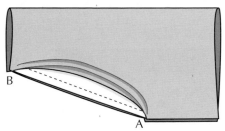

Stitch sleeves together at underarm; keep lining free.

5. Turn under the seam allowance on one lining edge and slipstitch it to the other to complete the sleeve.

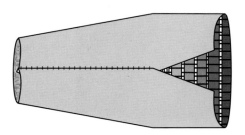

Slipstitch lining opening closed.

6. Position each sleeve on a vest front and the back, aligning the center of the top edge of the sleeve with the shoulder seam. Pin in place and try on. Adjust the sleeve position as needed for the desired sleeve length. Edgestitch the sleeve to the vest with straight stitching, or use a decorative stitch, such as the blanket stitch. Now your vest is a jacket!

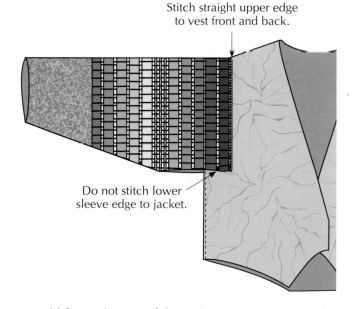

Stitch straight upper edge to vest front and back.

Do not stitch lower sleeve edge to jacket.

7. Add front closures if desired.

Check It Out

BY LORRAINE TORRENCE

For this machine-pieced and hand-appliquéd silk noil jacket, Lorraine modified a commercial pattern to create new areas for the piecing. Colorful appliquéd shapes provide more design movement and eye appeal.

Meet Lorraine Torrence

After earning a Master of Fine Arts degree in sculpture, Lorraine Torrence finally settled on her art medium of choice: fabric. She started teaching quiltmaking in 1972 and soon found uses for quiltmaking applications in garments. By 1985, Lorraine was in the wearable-art business, creating custom and production garments. Her wearables have been included in the prestigious Fairfield Fashion Show and have won First Place and Design Excellence awards in the American Quilter's Society Fashion Show and Contest.

Lorraine lives in Seattle, Washington, with her husband, Michael. They have two grown children. She teaches quiltmaking and wearable-art classes at In The Beginning, a quilt shop in Seattle, as well as at guilds and conferences nationwide. She is currently writing a book on design, to be published by That Patchwork Place.

Editor's Note:

Unlike other projects in this book, a specific pattern and yardages are not given for this garment. After you read Lorraine's thorough discussion of how she designed and sewed this ensemble, you will have the guidelines and information you need to design your own one-of-a-kind garment.

Her wish is that you tailor your design to fit a pattern that reflects your own personal sense of style and body type—not to duplicate her garment. Lorraine's sensible approach to the design process will help you make appropriate pattern and fabric selections for your project.

Choosing a Commercial Pattern

When I was a college freshman in a basic design class, our professor asked each of us to design an alphabet. "What's the most important thing about designing letters?" he asked. After we silently considered different answers ("they should be beautiful" or "they should be unique"), he answered the question for us: "They should be legible."

When I design a piece of wearable art, I remember my professor's practical advice and try to keep in mind my purpose in designing a garment. For me, the first requirement is that it fit properly and be wearable—that is, it should be comfortable, flattering, and appropriate for the occasion. Often, a commercial pattern is the best place to begin. Here's the process to follow:

1. Select a pattern that meets your needs for a basic shape. Look for simple, flat shapes that flatter your body type. However, if you have a curvy figure that requires a pattern with darts or princess seams for a good fit, select a pattern with shaping and plan your design for the pieced fabric to accommodate the darts or seams.
2. Take your measurements and compare them to the measurements given for different sizes.
3. Select a size that matches your measurements as closely as possible.
4. Make any alterations in the pattern you need to ensure a proper and flattering fit. Unless you do this first, all the time and effort invested in piecing, appliquéing, or otherwise embellishing the fabric will end in disappointment rather than satisfaction.

Note: *The pattern I chose has darts in the front and back. If your pattern does too, follow the suggestions in the Designer Tip on pages 91–92 for designing a stripe in a darted garment section.*

5. Lay a piece of tissue paper over the pattern drawing on the pattern envelope and trace it several times. This provides outlines for drawing design ideas in the next phase of your project.

Two possible designs   The final choice

Redesigning the Pattern

Often, I divide the pattern pieces into new areas for embellishment. There are two reasons for this.

- I believe that most good designs have areas that vary in their concentration of detail. Even totally blank spaces are legitimate, if not important, design elements. So, dividing a pattern piece to provide areas of dense embellishment that will contrast with plainer areas can be useful.

- Creating new pattern divisions in the shape makes matching pieced designs at construction seam lines easier. When I designed this project, I wanted a large checkerboard to flow over the right shoulder, onto the sleeve cap, and around to the back. On the other side, I wanted a smaller checkerboard to extend over the shoulder seam and onto the back but not onto the sleeve. I knew that, even with a considerable degree of skill in piecing, it would be hard to make the checkerboard match at the shoulder and sleeve seams. Eliminating these seams solved the problem.

Before you begin to redesign the actual pattern pieces to accommodate the new design:

1. Make any necessary pattern adjustments for your body.
2. Trace each adjusted pattern piece onto tissue paper, shelf paper, or doctor's examining-table paper, tracing a separate piece for each front, each sleeve, and the back pieces. If the back pattern piece is to be placed on a fold, be sure to trace a complete back, not just half of it.
3. Pin the pattern pieces together at any seam lines you want to eliminate. Remember, all pattern pieces must lie flat, just as they do in the original pattern. This means that the seams you eliminate must be straight lines.

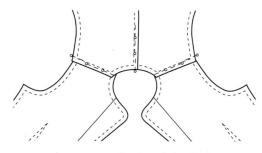

Pin pattern together at center back and shoulder seam lines. The combination lies flat because the seams are all straight lines.

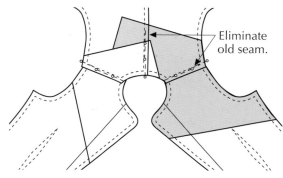

The shaded area becomes one of the new pattern pieces. The old seam lines in each new area are eliminated.

If a seam line is curved or shaped, you can cut a new shape only out of the part that is a straight line. Most of the center back seam on the pattern shown was not a straight line, so I only pinned the top part of the seam together (where it was a straight line). Remember, you can only eliminate a seam line and cut a new piece where the original seam is a straight line and does not provide shaping to the garment.

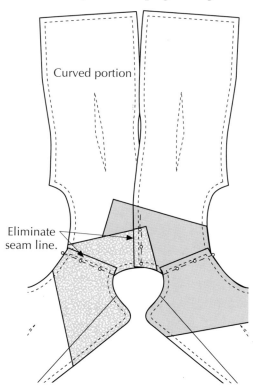

In redesigning the pattern for this project, I found a very high sleeve cap that required lots of easing to set it smoothly into the armhole. It helps to choose a sleeve cap that is somewhat flat to avoid a lot of easing. However, if you want to flatten a too-high sleeve cap, trim ⅛" from the top of the cap, tapering to nothing by the time you reach each armhole notch.

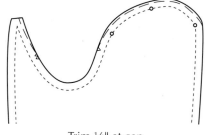

Trim ⅛" at cap.

If the sleeve still has too much fullness to smoothly ease the cap, you can safely trim another ⅛" from the top, again tapering to nothing at the notches.

Designer TIP

If you're new to making design changes in a pattern, test it in muslin or pattern tracing cloth before you actually use the new pattern piece to cut into your precious fabric.

4. Following your design drawing, draw the desired seam lines onto the pattern tissues. To integrate the design on the body of the garment with a set-in sleeve as I did, position the sleeve cap at the shoulder seam, with the shoulder dot at the shoulder seam line; pin it in place.

I wanted the right yoke to extend into the right sleeve. The lines on the right sleeve cap are continuations of the new yoke seam lines for the right front and back. For the left sleeve, I drew a seam line to separate the pieced section of the sleeve from the rest of it.

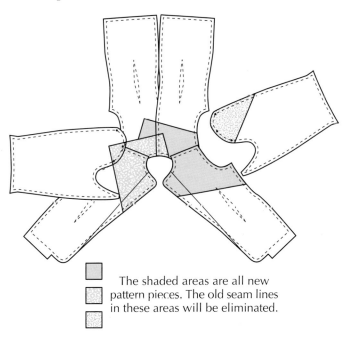

The shaded areas are all new pattern pieces. The old seam lines in these areas will be eliminated.

5. Cut the pattern apart on the new design lines and add a ¼"-wide seam allowance to each cut as shown for the pattern pieces.

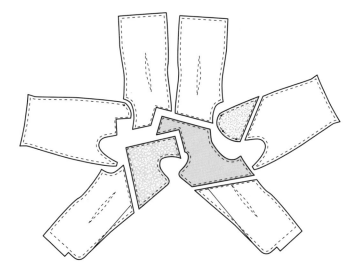

Determining Yardage Requirements

When you change a pattern and then add lots of piecing to make fabric for it, you will need to refigure the yardage requirements. If you are leaving some pattern pieces unchanged, lay these pieces out on a fabric similar in width to the one you want to purchase and determine the yardage for these pieces.

For the pieced areas, you will usually have enough fabric if you double the total amount it would normally take to cut those pattern pieces. Use this figure as a combined total figure for all the fabrics you want to use in the piecing, trying to imagine in what proportion you want to use each of them. For example, if it would take 2 yards to cut all the pattern pieces you intend to piece, double that to 4 yards, then divide proportionately among the different fabrics you want to use, such as 1 yard each of fabrics A and B, ¾ yard of C, ½ yard each of D and E, and ¼ yard of F. All this adds up to 4 yards. Don't forget to add what you need for the pattern pieces that don't require piecing.

Of course, you can always use the method perfected by experienced quilters—just buy a bunch of everything!

Checkerboard Piecing

To piece a checkerboard pattern, use the following strip-piecing method.

1. Cut strips of the 2 colors you've chosen to use in the desired finished width plus ½" for two ¼"-wide seam allowances. For example, for 2"-wide finished "checks," cut the strips 2½" wide.
2. Sew the strips together in the desired order, using ¼"-wide seam allowances. Press the seam allowances in one direction. Be sure to begin and end the strip set with different colors as shown.

Press.

3. From the completed strip set, cut strips the same width as you cut the strips.

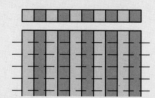

From the strip set, cut segments which are the size of the finished checkerboard you want plus ½". (This is the same measurement as the cut width of the original strips.)

4. Arrange the strips as shown so the colors alternate, checkerboard style, and sew them together, matching seams carefully. Press the seams in one direction.

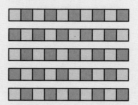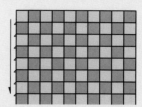

Note: For the lower front and back sections of this project, I pieced 2½"-wide strips (2"-wide finished) of dark green silk noil with 1"-wide strips (½"-wide finished) of light green silk noil. I also interrupted the wider dark green strips with ½"-wide strips of rainbow strip piecing. Note that the strips for the rainbow piecing were not all cut the same width, and I inserted some rainbow piecing into one of the light green strips for added drama.

1"

2½"

Rainbow pieced band for insert
Cut 1" segments.

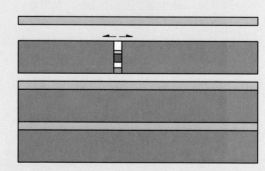

Piece 1"-wide segments of rainbow piecing into the 2½"-wide strips at selected places.

Making the Pieced Sections

After preparing the new pattern pieces, decide on the design you want to use to fill in the pieces. I chose a 2" (finished measurement of each square) checkerboard pattern for the right front, sleeve cap, and shoulder section. For the left front, shoulder, and back section, I wanted a slightly smaller checkerboard pattern (1¼" finished square). For the left sleeve, I used a ¾" finished square for the checkerboard pattern. If you want to use a checkerboard design in your garment, refer to "Checkerboard Piecing." Of course, you may choose some other piecing pattern for your design.

Piece enough fabric to accommodate the pattern pieces and cut them out.

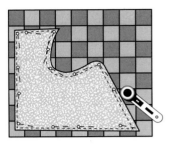

During the actual garment construction, remember that the seam allowances in your pieced sections are ¼" and the seam allowances in your garment are probably ⅝". (Check the pattern pieces.)

Designer TIP

Making a pieced stripe for a pattern piece is straightforward unless the piece has a dart. For the right front section of this project, I pieced enough striped fabric for the area above the dart, then added an extra large piece of the dark green to the bottom edge of the last light green strip. Next, I placed the pattern piece on the new "fabric" with the pieced section at the desired angle and cut out the piece 1" larger than the pattern piece as shown.

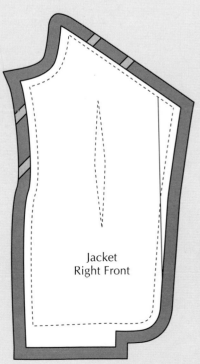

Jacket
Right Front

Next, I marked the dart, then stitched and pressed it as directed in the pattern instruction sheet.

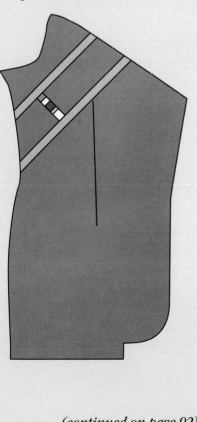

(continued on page 92)

(continued from page 91)

Finally, I made cuts across the darted area and inserted the remaining light green strips. Because the dart creates a piece that is no longer flat, it's important to smooth it out as much as possible when you make the cuts. Sometimes cutting like this creates a slight jog or dogleg in the resulting piece.

After I had pieced in as many stripes as I wanted, I placed my paper pattern (with the dart pinned into the paper) back on top of the pieced front, pinned the pattern carefully to the fabric (remember, it won't exactly lie flat because the dart is already sewn), and finished trimming the fabric to the size of the paper pattern.

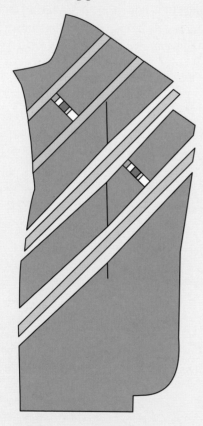

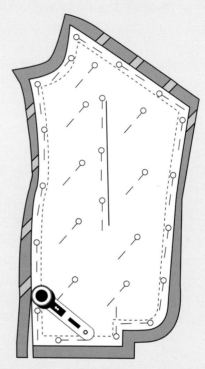

Trim the pieced section along pattern edges.

Note: Whenever you cut through an already pieced (or darted) fabric and use ¼"-wide seam allowances to insert a ½"-wide (finished) strip, the whole piece retains its original size and shape. That is why adding ½"-wide stripes in the body of the jacket allowed me to keep the shaping the dart provided. If I had pieced the stripes first and then sewn in the dart, the stripes might not have matched after the dart was sewn.

It's also important to carefully line up the dart seam lines when you insert the narrower strips.

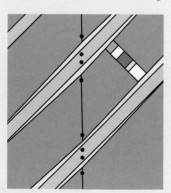

Matching Piecing from Section to Section

To continue a design from one section of a garment to another:

1. Piece one section, such as the lower right front, as previously described.
2. Place the paper pattern (with dart pinned in place) on top and trace all piecing seams.

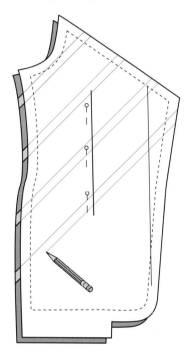

Trace piecing seams onto the pattern tissue.

3. Line up the marked paper-pattern piece with the pattern piece(s) for the adjoining section(s). If you are lining up the two fronts, overlap and align the center front lines of both pieces.
4. With a pencil, place a mark on the second pattern piece where the piecing lines on the first pattern piece end at the seam line. These lines will enable you to continue the piecing design for perfectly matched seams and to make the transition from one piece to the next.

   I usually make one piece, mark the edge of the piece next to it, and then finish piecing that piece. I continue in this fashion until the pattern pieces for all adjoining pieces are marked. Finally, I design some way to connect the two edges on the last piece to complete the design.

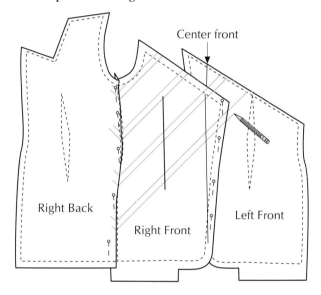

Center front

Right Back

Right Front

Left Front

Designer TIP

Wearable art requires designing for a three-dimensional surface. Making a design continue and connect all the way around results in a more successful piece than one in which the design on the front stops at the shoulder and side seams.

Making designs only on the front of vests may have started when designers simply mimicked the vests of men's traditional three-piece suits. The backs of men's vests were made of lining material because only the fronts were designed to be seen. If you plan for the back of your garment to be seen, why not design it too!

Constructing the Garment

You are ready to assemble your garment after you have pieced and/or embellished each piece. Generally, I follow the pattern instructions for the garment I've chosen, with the following exceptions:

- Even garments meant to be unlined will need to be lined to conceal and protect the piecing seams. You have two options: line the garment in the traditional manner to completely conceal all piecing and construction seams, or make an underlining. If you choose the latter, you must cut a piece of underlining for each garment piece and baste it to the wrong side, then construct the garment as if the two layers were one. You will have exposed construction seams, which you may need to finish to prevent raveling.

- Grain line often gets ignored in the piecing process, as when straight-of-grain strips fall diagonally in the finished garment. Try to keep major parts of the garment on the straight of grain. If that's not possible, it may be best to do your piecing on a lightweight, straight-of-grain foundation, such as preshrunk muslin.

- The new seam lines you've added when stitching the pieced sections may require changes in the assembly order given on the pattern instruction sheet.

In "Check It Out," I sewed the lower jacket body together all the way around, matching the piecing seams at each major seam line; then I sewed the right sleeve together (remember there was a chunk taken out of it at the top, which is now part of the shoulder section) and set it into the partial sleeve opening available to it.

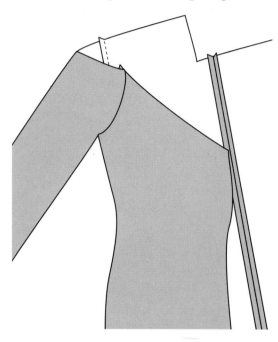

Because I edged the checkerboard parts with piping, and the seams turned corners, it was easier to turn under and press the piped-yoke seam allowance, then lap it over the lower jacket sections and stitch in-the-ditch to secure it. I used thread that matched the piping.

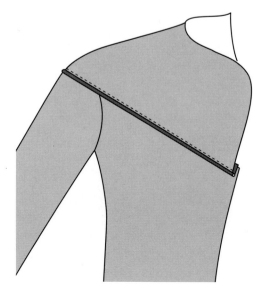

- When the pattern requires interfacing, I often use the fusible variety because it's so convenient. However, when interfacing is fused onto a pieced surface, the seam allowances show in distinct relief on the right side of the garment—an undesirable effect. To avoid this, I fuse the interfacing to the facing or lining instead of the outer garment itself, or I use sew-in interfacing.
- When you need to add practical features, such as pockets or buttons and buttonholes, to your wearable-art garment, think of these areas as opportunities to enhance or continue the design theme.

I added a rainbow-pieced welt pocket in the blank area on the lower part of the left front and placed it at an angle that echoed the piped edges of the checkerboard yoke. (For welt-pocket instructions, consult a pattern instruction sheet or a tailoring book.)

After your garment is assembled, you may want to add embellishments. My own rule of thumb is: Do only as much as the piece needs—and do it tastefully. Some wearable art looks wonderful when it is encrusted with threads, beads, bangles, and manipulated fabric. To my eye, "Check It Out" needed only some floating shapes in the same silk noil, repeating the colors in the rainbow-pieced inserts. The curvilinear shapes were made by cutting true-bias strips, pressing under the raw edges, and coaxing them into the new shapes with the iron. They were appliquéd to the jacket before the lining was added.

Sources

You may order garment patterns specified in this book from the following sources.

Judy Bishop Designs
24603 Island Avenue, Department B
Carson, CA 90745

The Panel Vest is $11.50 postage paid. Send a check or money order in U.S. funds only. Ask for her brochure on other patterns in her line suitable for wearables.

Lois Ericson
Design and Sew Patterns
PO Box 5222, Salem, OR 97304

Woven Vests #314 is $12.00 postage paid. Send a check or money order in U.S. funds only. Lois's book, *Opening & Closing,* is available for $32.00 postage paid.

Maggie Walker
3 Buck Run Drive
Elverson, PA 19520
610-469-0891

The Vintage Vest is $11.50 postage paid. Send a check or money order in U.S. funds only. Call to charge with Visa or MasterCard. Ask for her brochure on other wearable patterns.

Dana Bontrager
Purrfection Artistic Wearables
19618 Canyon Drive
Granite Falls, WA 98252
360-691-4293

PAW Prints Designs #007 Kimono Jacket and Vest is $11.95 postage paid. Send a check or money order in U.S. funds only. Ask for her brochure on other wearable patterns.

Publications and Products

Many titles are available at your local quilt shop.
For more information, write for a free color catalog
to That Patchwork Place, Inc., PO Box 118, Bothell,
WA 98041-0118 USA.

☎ U.S. and Canada, call **1-800-426-3126** for the
name and location of the quilt shop nearest you.
Int'l: 1-425-483-3313   Fax: 1-425-486-7596
E-mail: info@patchwork.com
Web: www.patchwork.com   10.97